Religion, Dress and the Body

Dress, Body, Culture

Series Editor **Joanne B. Eicher**, *Regents' Professor, University of Minnesota*

Advisory Board:

Ruth Barnes, *Ashmolean Museum, University of Oxford*
Helen Callaway, *CCCRW, University of Oxford*
James Hall, *University of Illinois at Chicago*
Beatrice Medicine, *California State University, Northridge*
Ted Polhemus, *Curator, "Street Style" Exhibition, Victoria & Albert Museum*
Griselda Pollock, *University of Leeds*
Valerie Steele, *The Museum at the Fashion Institute of Technology*
Lou Taylor, *University of Brighton*
John Wright, *University of Minnesota*

Books in this provocative series seek to articulate the connections between culture and dress which is defined here in its broadest possible sense as any modification or supplement to the body. Interdisciplinary in approach, the series highlights the dialogue between identity and dress, cosmetics, coiffure, and body alternations as manifested in practices as varied as plastic surgery, tattooing, and ritual scarification. The series aims, in particular, to analyze the meaning of dress in relation to popular culture and gender issues and will include works grounded in anthropology, sociology, history, art history, literature, and folklore.

ISSN: 1360-466X

Previously published titles in the Series

Helen Bradley Foster, *"New Raiments of Self": African American Clothing in the Antebellum South*
Claudine Griggs, *"S/he: Changing Sex and Changing Clothes"*
Michaele Thurgood Haynes, *Dressing Up Debutantes: Pageantry and Glitz in Texas*
Dani Cavallaro and Alexandra Warwick, *Fashioning the Frame: Boundaries, Dress and the Body*
Judith Perani and Norma H. Wolff (eds), *Cloth, Dress and Art Patronage in Africa*

DRESS, BODY, CULTURE

Religion, Dress and the Body

Linda B. Arthur

Oxford • New York

First published in 1999 by
Berg
Editorial offices:
150 Cowley Road, Oxford, OX4 1JJ, UK
70 Washington Square South, New York, NY 10012, USA

Berg is an imprint of Oxford International Publishers Ltd.

Library of Congress Cataloging-in-Publication Data
A catalog record for this book is available from the Library of Congress.

British Library Cataloguing-in-Publication Data
A catalogue record for this book is available from the British Library.

ISBN   1 85973 292 5 (Cloth)
           1 85973 297 6 (Paper)

Typeset by JS Typesetting, Wellingborough, Northants.
Printed and bound in Great Britain by
Biddles Ltd, Guildford and King's Lynn

Contents

Contents

Acknowledgements

This volume has its genesis in both my personal and professional upbringing. To my parents Tony and Jean Gehringer, who taught me to appreciate religion and culture and to simultaneously think and question, I owe a tremendous debt. My husband, Peter Arthur, is a wonderful editor and critic, and he and my sons Joel and Brendan keep me continually analyzing the 'why' of social behavior and the power of institutions in everyday life. Mentors and colleagues Peg Rucker, Susan Kaiser, Jean Hamilton and Marcia Morgado have helped me enormously to focus on the ideological underpinnings of peoples' behavior with regard to dress.

I am grateful to several people for their help in bringing this volume to print: Joanne Eicher and Kathryn Earle both encouraged me to develop this anthology, as well as an upcoming volume on religion, the body and dress from a cross-cultural perspective. Twelve anonymous reviewers provided helpful insights and suggestions as the chapters were submitted to blind peer-review; they are to be commended for their devotion to the referee process that evidences a selfless devotion to quality scholarship.

Finally, I thank all of the people who provided information for the studies that led to the chapters in this volume. Due to the promise of anonymity that we ethnographers and qualitative researchers make to our informants, these people cannot be named. They are, however, the most vital aspect of the research; their interest in, and cooperation with the researcher ensures the reliability and validity of qualitative research.

Notes on Contributors

Karen Anijar is Assistant Professor in the Department of Curriculum and Instruction at Arizona State University. Her research focuses on both cultural studies and educational curricula. She is the author of numerous articles and chapters on Curriculum and Cultural Studies. Dr Anijar is the author of two forthcoming books: *Teaching Towards the Twenty-Forth Century: The Curriculum of Star Trek*, and *Paying Attention: The Political Economy of Nurture*.

Linda B. Arthur is Associate Professor of Textiles and Clothing and Curator of the Historic Costume Collection at the University of Hawai'i at Manoa. Her research explores the intersection of gender, ethnicity and ideology, and the impact of these social locations on women's appearance. While her numerous publications in the past two decades have been on exclusive groups and ethno-religious groups in the United States, Dr Arthur 's current research focus is on ethnicity and identity in Asia and the Pacific. Dr Arthur has two forthcoming books, which include another volume in this series (on religion, culture and dress from a cross-cultural perspective) and a book on Hawaiian dress.

Barbara Goldman Carrel is Adjunct Assistant Professor at the City University of New York. Her research on Hasidic women's clothing intersects the boundary of fashion and folk costume, exploring issues of identity, ethnicity and status. Ultimately, she questions the artificial divide between fashion and folk costume. She received her BA in Anthropology from the University of Pennsylvania, and an MA in Library Science from Drexel University, as well as an MA in Anthropology from New York University.

Catherine Daly is Assistant Professor in the Department of Textiles, Clothing and Design at the University of Nebraska. Her research interests include clothing and human behavior and women's textile arts, with particular regional focus on women of Islamic affiliation in Central and South Asia. A Fulbright Scholar in 1998 at the National College of Arts in Lahore, Pakistan, Dr Daly taught in the Textile Design Department and conducted research among Afghan refugee women in Peshawar. Using qualitative and reflexive research methods she explores the geopolitics of gender, ethnic identity and religious affiliation.

Sandra Lee Evenson is Assistant Professor of Clothing, Textiles and Design in the Margaret Ritchie School of Family and Consumer Sciences at the University of Idaho. She earned her BS, MS, and PhD at the University of Minnesota. Her teaching and research interests include Indian trade textiles, cultural aspects of dress, and apparel product development. She is currently co-authoring a revision of *The Visible Self: Cultural Perspectives on Dress* with Joanne B. Eicher and Hazel A. Lutz, and serves on the board of the Northwest Sewn Products Association. She lives in Pullman, Washington.

Gayle Veronica Fischer is Assistant Professor in the History Department of Salem State College, and teaches world history and gender history. Fischer has written articles on dress reform for a number of journals, including *Communal Studies, Mid-America,* and *Feminist Studies.* She has recently completed a manuscript on nineteenth-century dress reform movements in the US and is completing an encyclopedia on clothing and social history in the United States. Her next project will examine formal and informal regulations of appearance.

Beth Graybill is Adjunct Professor of Women's Studies at Franklin and Marshal College while completing her PhD in American Studies at the University of Maryland at College Park. Her research to date has investigated dress and gender among conservative Mennonites. Other research interests include women, religion and ethnography. She lives in Lancaster, Pennsylvania with her husband and son.

Jean A. Hamilton is Associate Professor, Department of Textiles and Apparel Management, University of Missouri-Columbia. Dr Hamilton's scholarship centers on the cultural system as the level of analysis in investigations of ethnographic, historical, and contemporary dress. She is respected both for her commitment to highlighting the importance of dress in social life from a cultural perspective and for her use of qualitative research methods, which she teaches, as the means for investigating the use of dress in cultural systems. Dr Hamilton has written several articles that serve as the foundation of much of the research being done by clothing and textiles scholars who are committed to cultural analysis.

Jana M. Hawley is Assistant Professor, School of Merchandising and Hospitality Management, University of North Texas in Denton. Dr Hawley's research interests are focused on economic activity related to behaviors and meanings associated with dress approached from a cultural perspective. Her work with the Amish serves as a model for examining the dynamic between economy and other competitive aspects of cultural systems. She is particularly focused on issues related to international trade, entrepreneurship, and production, distribution and consumption, all as they relate to dress.

Susan Michelman is Associate Professor of Consumer Studies at the University of Massachusetts at Amherst. Her research and teaching focus on issues of dress and identity and she has published numerous articles on this subject. Currently, she is co-editing a forthcoming textbook titled *Meanings of Dress*.

Gwendolyn O'Neal is Associate Professor, Department of Consumer and Textile Sciences, The Ohio State University. Her recent research has focused on documenting an African American aesthetic of dress. Dr O'Neal's work has linked the elements of the African American aesthetic to slave dress and to that found in West African cultures during the slave trade era.

David Trayte is Assistant Professor in Clothing, Textiles and Design in the Margaret Ritchie School of Family and Consumer Sciences at the University of Idaho. He has a BA in psychology from Doane College in Crete Nebraska; an MA in Textiles, Clothing and Design from the University of Nebraska at Lincoln and a PhD in Design, Housing and Apparel from the University of Minnesota. His teaching and research interests include the socio-cultural, psychological and historic aspects of textiles and clothing. He lives in Pullman, Washington.

Frank A. Salamone is Professor of Sociology and Anthropology at Iona College, New Rochelle, New York. He has published extensively on Nigeria, Ghana and other areas in Africa. He has also published on Italian-Americans in Rochester, New York. Recently, he has begun to publish on jazz, literature and popular culture. The Polynesian Cultural Center is central to his work on presentation of identity in public areas, especially in tourist sites. Salamone has published over 150 articles and chapters in books and written or edited ten books. He has recently completed *Art and Leisure* and is working on *Jazz and Popular Culture*.

List of Illustrations

Introduction: Dress and the Social Control of the Body

Linda B. Arthur

Dress provides a window through which we might look into a culture, because it visually attests to the salient ideas, concepts and categories fundamental to that culture. Age, gender, ethnicity and religion help to define a person's social location and are made visible when cultures make dress salient, as it is in all of the American religious groups presented in this volume. The term 'dress' is used in the most global sense to refer to all of the ways the body is used in the expression of identity. Dress is the most obvious of the many symbolic boundary markers used by conservative religious groups. This book examines how the metaphor of appearance is used within religious groups in the United States to simultaneously express religiosity, ethnicity and gender norms. In many of the most conservative groups, we will see that dress codes are used as gender norms that reinforce the existing power system.

Through conformance to a strict religious value system, the most conservative of the religious social bodies exert control over their members' physical bodies. Since strict conformity is equated with religiosity, compliance to strict codes of behavior is demanded. The internal body is controlled, in that emotion is restrained, voices and laughter are muffled and appetite for food, knowledge and sex are constrained. The external body, however, is more visibly restrained. Strict dress codes are enforced because dress is considered symbolic of religiosity. Hence, dress becomes a symbol of social control as it controls the external body. While a person's level of religiosity can not be objectively perceived, symbols such as clothing are used as evidence that s/he is on the 'right and true path.'

The Social Control of the Body

Although the body is central to personal identity, social interaction and thus society at large, the body has been relatively neglected in sociology (Synnott,

1993). The sociology of the body is in its infancy; this new area of sociological research attempts to study the self as embodied, the body as a symbolic system (Shilling, 1993). Behavioral and dress codes are used in conservative religious groups as symbols of religiosity and social control. This follows Douglas's (1966) argument that 'the body provides a basic theme for all symbolism' (p. 163–4).

Mary Douglas (1966, 1970) pioneered the study of the body as a symbol of the social order. Goffman (1963, 1971) followed with his examination of the management of the body in social interaction and showed the body as central to human agency. Fueled by the writings of Michel Foucault (1974, 1979, 1980), scholarship that examined the human body as a vehicle of social inquiry began to proliferate during the 1980s. Foucault (1974) saw the body as governed by political systems and focused on an epistemological view of the body as existing in discourse. Foucault noted that the soul is more than an ideological construct; it exists and has a reality in that it is produced within, around and on the body (1979). The cases presented in this volume illustrate Foucault's notion that the soul is both real and produced *on* the body through a dynamic system of power relationships between individuals, their bodies and cultures. Burroughs and Erenreich (1993) showed that social systems stamp messages about the dynamics of power relationships onto individuals' bodies as the process of the social construction of the body in turn creates culture. To use Bourdieu's own language, ' the social determinations attached to a determinate position in the social space tend, through relationship to one's own body, to shape the dispositions constituting social identity' (1990, p. 71).

Pierre Bourdieu's (1973) theory of social reproduction has at its very heart a concern for the body as a bearer of symbolic value. The body, for Bourdieu, is an unfinished entity that develops in conjunction with various social forces and is integral to the maintenance of social inequalities. As a natural phenomenon that both constitutes and is constituted by society, analysis of the body is a necessary component of post-modern social life. The body is constantly affected by social, cultural and economic processes. Social groups adopt a particular style of dress in relation to the meanings given to alternative styles, the orientation to the body that style of dress encourages and to the relationship between the fields of fashion and other social fields (Bourdieu, 1973).

For this book, however, Bryan Turner's work is most relevant and illuminating. The sociology of the body turns out to be, according to Turner (1984, p. 114) 'crucially about the control of female sexuality by men exercising patriarchal power.' Turner argues that every society must solve the Hobbesian problem of order and to do so means to solve four problems, two of which concern the political body in terms of reproduction and regulation, both considered by Turner to be 'political problems.' At the 'individual body' level (the focus of this book), the two problems Turner cites are the need for restraint of desire, a problem of the internal body; and the importance of representation of bodies to each other, a problem of the external body (Synnott, 1993). Turner, then, provides a model for analysis of the social control of dress and thus for this book.

The investigation of dress as a vital component of the social control system of cultures is, unfortunately, rarely the topic of research. This book seeks to address that void in the literature.

Dress Codes and Social Control

Dress includes both body supplements, such as clothing and accessories and behaviors, such as dieting, plastic surgery and cosmetics, leading to changes in body shape. Holistically, then, dress functions as an effective means of non-verbal communication during social interaction; it influences the establishment and projection of identity (Roach-Higgins and Eicher, 1992).

That dress is a visible manifestation of cultural values is well known, as dress code research tends to show (Davis, 1989; Hall, 1993; Lipp, 1989; Rivere, 1992). In examining the effects of conformity to gender-role expectations for dress, Workman and Johnson (1994) found that evaluations of individuals were influenced by perceptions of deviance from expected norms. Similarly, Micklin (1977) found low tolerance for marginal behavior and deviant dress, leading to the exercise of social control.

Research on social control tends to be macroscopic in nature and focuses on the use of formal or legal means of control. Goffman (1963) reminded us that symbols operate at the microscopic level of normative social control. Normative social control begins with personal social control through self-regulation, followed by informal social control. When the individual begins to offend, peers may disapprove and pressure the individual to conform to the norms. Finally, the threat that an offender introduces to the social order is managed through formal social control measures, administered by specialized agents. Thus, norms are managed through social control to inhibit deviation and insure conformity to social norms at even the most minute level (Goffman, 1971).

Through symbolic devices, the physical body exhibits the normative values of the social body (Douglas, 1982). Symbols, such as dress, help delineate the social unit and visually define its boundaries because they give non-verbal information about the individual. Unique dress attached to specific cultural groups, then, can function to insulate group members from outsiders, while bonding the members to each other. Normative behavior within the culture re-affirms loyalty to the group and can be evidenced by the wearing of a uniform type of attire (Joseph, 1986).

Social Control in Ethno-religious Communities

Within complex urban societies there are specific ethno-religious groups that intentionally separate themselves from the rest of society and attempt to re-establish the small, face-to-face community. Mennonites, Hutterites and Amish are such groups. The perception of the Old Order Amish as a deviant religious group was found by Thompson (1986) to be related more to their deviant behaviors, visually manifest in dress, than to their religious differences from mainstream Christianity. An essential factor in ethno-religious groups, social control has not received much attention in ethnographic literature. A notable exception was the work done by Soloman Poll (1962) on the Hasidic community in Williamsburg, New York. Poll pointed to social control as significant in terms of the survival prospects of the group. Among these orthodox Jews, social control was achieved in ways remarkably similar to those used by the Holdemans. The most salient features included isolation from the external society; emphasis on conformity with status related to religiosity, symbolized by clothing status markers; a powerful rabbinical organization and rigorous sanctions to insure conformity to norms.

Goffman (1971) suggests that research into symbolic behavior is best accomplished through qualitative methods and ethnographic fieldwork. The contributors to this volume and I wholeheartedly support this approach, because often times people engage in symbolic behavior without a conscious understanding of why they do what they do. At the beginning of my research in the mid-1970s I asked a Holdeman Mennonite woman why the women in her community dress much like their foremothers did a century earlier. The answer I received was that 'It has always been so.' The answer to this question eluded me until I learned ethnographic fieldwork techniques because symbols operate beneath the conscious level and often cannot be verbally articulated. Answering the question of why the Holdeman women dressed as they did took eight years of fieldwork and yielded incredibly rich data. When the topics are sensitive and complex, as research into dress usually is, qualitative and ethnographic methods yield data with great depth.

All of the authors in *Religion, Dress and the Body* used either qualitative or ethnographic methods in order to understand the relationships between the visual manifestation of religio-cultural practices in the dress of religious groups in the United States. Religion can also control bodies invisibly, as noted in the chapters by Hamilton and Hawley, in their research on Mormons and the Amish and by Graybill and Arthur, in their fieldwork with Mennonite communities.

Fossilized fashion has been explained as a sudden 'freezing' of fashion whereby a group continues to wear a style long after it has become outmoded for the general population. This phenomenon has been explained as expressing dignity and high social status (Laver, 1969), or the group's religious, old-fashioned, sectarian identity (Gordon, 1986). While the connection between fossilized fashion and ethnicity within religious groups might seem apparent, it has only recently been addressed in the literature (Arthur, 1998). This book will show, however, that within certain ethno-religious groups, fossilized fashion is used in contemporary settings as a visual symbol of traditional gender roles for women; this generally occurs in societies that find change to be a threat. The chapters on the Amish, Mennonites and Hasidic Jews in this volume substantiate this use of fossilized fashion.

Bush and London (1960) noted that traditional gender roles can be marked by a particular form of dress where the roles are stable for long periods of time; further, they noted that when dress changes suddenly in these groups, we can expect to find a change in gender roles. The chapter on Women Religious in this volume shows that the habit changed as the nun's roles within the Church changed. In further elaboration of Bush and London's hypothesis, I would also note that when roles are restrictive, we can expect to see a restriction in women's dress, in the form of either dress codes or physically restrictive clothing. Many of the chapters in this volume elucidate the variety of dress codes created for women living within patriarchal societies.

Several chapters in this volume focus on the distinction between the sacred and the profane, especially in the symbolic separation of the ethno-religious subculture from a dominant culture. In addition, the relationship between patriarchy and the social control of women is also found in these chapters. Carrel's work on Orthodox Jewish women; Daly's fieldwork on Afghani women in the Midwest; Fisher's research on Strangite Mormons; Hamilton and Hawley's work comparing Amish and the LDS Mormons and Graybill and Arthur's fieldwork on Mennonites all show that the binary opposition of the sacred and the profane are intentionally used to visually separate these religious groups from the larger culture. In doing so, these patriarchal societies intentionally use dress codes to maintain a gendered imbalance of power.

The role of dress in visually exhibiting the acculturation of indigenous people and immigrants is a theme throughout several chapters in this volume. Carrel and Anijar both discuss the immigration of European Jews to America, although they each examine different ends of the acculturation continuum. Carrel's work on the Hasidic Jews, who chose to reflect their ethnicity by retaining fossilized fashion, is contrasted with Anijar's chapter on the larger body of Jews in America who used dress to assimilate into the larger American culture.

No volume on dress and religion would be complete without a discussion of the role of Christian missionaries in the acculturation process. Missionaries advanced their own ethnocentric perceptions of appropriate behavior and dress and, often through subtle coertion, guided the acculturation of indigenous peoples. Evenson and Trayte examined this topic with regard to nineteenth-century Dakota in Minnesota and Salamone analyzes the contemporary Mormon impact on Polynesians in his chapter on the Polynesian Cultural Center in Hawai'i.

The relationship between religion, culture and dress is not always constraining. Freedom to assert a changed identity within an ethno-religious subculture is the theme of three chapters. Dress was used as a means of negotiating a new social environment as well, within these religious groups. O'Neal examines the role of dress in the Black Church as a means of positive ethnic identification. Anijar discusses the use of dress by mainstream Jews as they assimilated into American culture and Michelman analyzes a unique event in the lives of Catholic nuns, who relinquished religious habits for secular dress after significant structural changes in the Church. In this chapter, Michelman shows that the increase in personal freedom for nuns led to a realignment of their personal and social identities.

While dress is commonplace, it is not ephemeral, vacuous or meaningless. We wear our identities on our bodies and our bodies are used by religions to visually communicate world views. *Religion, Dress and the Body* draws attention to the complexity of meanings surrounding dress and to the ways that bodies can be read as communicating social and religious values. This book explores the ways in which the sacred dress of religious groups is used in a social hierarchy of religiosity to facilitate social and ideological agendas. It sheds light on the use of the body as a cultural symbol used in expressing, establishing and maintaining (1) personal and social identities, (2) social hierarchies, (3) definitions of deviance, (4) systems of social control and (5) patriarchal power in ethno-religious subcultures. As a consequence, then, this book shows that the ethno-religious body is both 'material and metaphor' (Turner, 1996, p. 43), the result of both functional and discursive changes that have arisen out of economic, political and historical exigencies. The body, then, is mutable; it is constantly changing; it is continually in process. To use Turner's words, the body is the most 'proximate and immediate feature of the social self' (Turner, 1996 p. 43).

References

Arthur, L. B. (1998). Fossilized fashion in Hawai'i. *Paideusis; Journal of Interdisciplinary Cultural Studies (1).* A15–28.

Bourdieu, P. (1990). *The logic of practice.* Stanford: Stanford University Press.

Bourdieu, P. (1973). Cultural reproduction and social reproduction, in R. Brown (ed.) *Knowledge, education and social change.* London: Tavistock.

Bush, G. and London, P. (1960). On the disappearance of knickers: Hypotheses for the functional analysis of the psychology of clothing. *American Journal of Sociology, 51:* 359–366.

Burroughs, C. B. and Erenreich, J. D. (1993). *Reading the social body.* Iowa City, IA: University of Iowa Press.

Davis, F. (1989). Of maids' uniforms and blue jeans: The drama of status ambivalences in clothing and fashion. *Qualitative sociology, 12* (1). Winter. 337–355.

Douglas, M. (1966). *Purity and danger.* London: Routledge.

Douglas, M. (1970). *Body symbols.* Oxford: Blackstone.

Douglas, M. (1982). *Natural symbols.* New York: Pantheon Books.

Foucault, M. (1974). *The archaeology of knowledge.* London: Tavistock.

Foucault, M. (1979) *Discipline and punish: The birth of the prison.* Trans. by Alan Sheridan. Harmondsworth: Penguin.

Foucault, M. (1980). *The history of sexuality Vol. 1; an introduction.* Trans. Robert Hurley. NY: Vintage Books.

Goffman, E. (1963). *Stigma: Notes on the management of spoiled identity.* Englewood Cliffs, NJ: Prentice-Hall.

Goffman, E. (1971). *Relations in public.* New York: Harper and Row.

Hall, E. (1993). Waitering/waitressing: Engendering the work of table servers. *Gender and Society, 7* (3). Sept. 329–45.

Joseph, N. (1986). *Uniforms and non-uniforms.* Westport, CT: Greenwood.

Lipp, S. (1989). Racial and ethnic problems: Peru. *International Journal of Group Tensions, 19* (1). Winter. 339–48.

Micklin, M. (1977). Anticipated reactions to deviance in a South American city: A study of social control. *Pacific Sociological Review, 20* (19) Oct. 515–35.

Poll, S. (1962). *The Hasidic community in Williamsburg.* NY: Glance Free Press.

Rivere, C. (1992). The rite of enchanting harmony; El rite enchantant la concorde. *Cahiers Internationaux de Sociologie, 39* (92). Jan–June, 5–29.

Roach-Higgins, M. and Eicher, J. (1992). Dress and identity. *Clothing and Textiles Research Journal, 10* (1), 1–8.

Shilling, C. (1993). *The body and social theory.* London: Sage.

Synnott, A. (1993). *The body social.* London: Routledge.

Thompson, W. (1986). Deviant ideology: The case of the Old Order Amish. *Quarterly Journal of Ideology, 10* (1). Jan. 29–33.

Turner, B. (1984). *Body and society.* Oxford: Basil Blackwell.

Workman, J. and Johnson, K. (1991). Effects of conformity and non-conformity to gender-role expectations for dress: Teachers versus students. *Adolescence, 29* (113). Spring, 207–23.

2

The Social Control of Women's Bodies in Two Mennonite Communities

Beth Graybill and Linda B. Arthur

I can say that in this kind of dressing, I found my role. . . . For years and years I was looking for something to express that I was a Christian woman . . . and once I came here and they gave me some dresses, I thought, 'Oh, now I'm living how Christ wants me to live.' (Kristina)[1]

For quite some time, Leah was in 'church trouble.' She was ill, spiritually ill. She was [eventually] expelled for having 'foreign spirits.' We could all see it in her behavior and her dress; she was just out of control. (Sarah)

The use of symbolic boundary markers has long been a practice of conservative Mennonite groups. Visual symbols, particularly dress, provide a window through which one can examine the operant social control system. This chapter examines metaphors of women's appearance and their use by two conservative Mennonite communities to evaluate conformity to socio-religious norms and to provide for both informal and formal measures of social control within these 'plain' communities.

The quotes that begin this chapter illustrate the relationship between women's dress, identity expression and Mennonite church standards of social control. Dress visually testifies to a woman's spiritual state in conservative Mennonite groups. Unfortunately, the investigation of dress as a vital component of the social control system of cultures is rarely the topic of research. The term 'dress' is used in the most global sense to refer to all of the ways in which the body expresses identity, including not only clothing, but accessories, grooming and the shaping of the body. Holistically, then, dress functions as an effective means of non-verbal communication during social interaction.

Dress influences the establishment and projection of identity, especially gender (Roach-Higgins and Eicher, 1992). Moreover, dress encourages women to internalize a prescribed set of gendered expectations for behavior (Eicher and Roach-Higgins, 1992).

Through conformance to a strict religious value system, the Mennonite social body exerts control over women's dress and the presentation of their physical bodies. Normative social control takes three forms. First, there is personal social control, illustrated by Kristina, above. The individual refrains from improper behavior by self-regulation. Second, there is informal social control. When the individual begins to offend, peers issue a warning of disapproval. Negative peer pressure may consolidate against an individual, as in Sarah's quote, above. Alternately, increasing peer pressure may eventually bring the offender into line, thus reaffirming social norms (Goffman, 1971). Third, the offender's threat to the social order is managed through formal social control, with social sanctions administered by specialized agents. In sum, personal, informal and formal control are the means by which conformity to social norms is effected. Deviation is inhibited or corrected and compliance is thus assured (Goffman, 1971).

As we explore below, in the conservative Mennonite context, a woman's internal body is controlled in that emotion is restrained and appetites for knowledge and sex are constrained. Her external body is more visibly restricted, however, because dress is considered symbolic of religiosity. While a woman's level of religious piety cannot be objectively perceived, symbols such as clothing are used as evidence that she is on the 'right and true path'. Consequently, appearance is constantly scrutinized. If she deviates from the dress and behavioral codes, a woman is defined as deviant and subjected to a number of formal and informal constraints. Mennonite women (and their clothing) are controlled by each other, by their men and by their ministers. Succinctly stated by Becky, a 23 year-old Mennonite woman, 'when I put on Mennonite clothing, I put on all of the Church's rules.' Hence dress becomes a potent symbol of social control.

Research Setting and Methods

Prior to entering the field, thorough research into published materials on conservative Mennonites was conducted. Mennonite archives provided material of limited circulation in order to provide historical background to the study. Each researcher investigated the archival documents pertaining to the group she was to study, with particular focus on the topics of discipline and gender.

Relying primarily on ethnographic interviews, data for this chapter was gathered during lengthy ethnographic investigations in two conservative Mennonite communities on opposite sides of the United States. In addition, each was in different geographic settings – one in rural Northern California, the other in suburban Eastern Pennsylvania.

Bend, a tiny river town in Northern California, is a farming community of Holdeman Mennonites.[2] Large families of about five children are the norm and raising children as good Christians is the central focus of all. The community is comprised of 350 individuals in sixty-five families who live patrilocally. It is common for several generations of a man's family to live on farms near each other because land is inherited patrilineally.

Beyond Bend, the community has extensive interaction with Holdeman congregations in California and other mid-western states. The communities are linked through marriage as well, since the Holdemans are religiously endogamous. Approximately half of the young women leave Bend to marry men from other congregations. The combination of endogamy, patrilocal residence and a rarity of converts creates a community in which most people are related (at least distantly) to each other.

The current research follows Arthur's earlier ethnographic work on the Bend congregation (Boynton, 1986; Arthur, 1992, 1997). Participant observation fieldwork included attendance at church services, Sunday school meetings, school classrooms, weddings, potluck dinners, youth group activities, quilting bees and numerous informal gatherings in women's homes. Most of the data was collected through casual interviews and focus group interviews of women aged from sixteen to seventy-five.

By contrast, adult members of the Eastern Pennsylvania Mennonite Church number about 3,500, primarily in eastern and north-central Pennsylvania. Over a period of four years, in-depth interviews were conducted with women from three church districts in and around Lancaster County, Pennsylvania; the women interviewed ranged in age from twenty-four to eighty-two. Church bishops and single women who had left the denomination were also interviewed. Graybill also relied on participant observation in homes, church-run stores, family reunions and church services.

Among Eastern Pennsylvania Mennonites, families of four to seven children are the norm (Mary, one informant, described her family of five children as 'small, but that's because we married late'). Although rural dwellers, less than 25 percent of the families in the church districts where Graybill conducted interviews continue to farm. Most men are employed in various blue-collar trades while married women, as in the Holdeman community, are occupied full-time at home in the domestic sphere. Religious endogamy is required of members.

On a continuum of plainness, Eastern Pennsylvania Mennonites rub shoulders with both Amish and more and less conservative Mennonites. Because these groups have been marketed as a valuable tourist commodity, interactions with tourists as well as with other Amish or Mennonite groups prevent the insularity found in a more homogenous community such as Bend.

In lifestyle and beliefs, Holdeman Mennonites and Eastern Pennsylvania Mennonites share much in common, though neither group fellowships with the other, owing largely to differing geographical and historical factors. The two groups both accept electricity, telephones and automobiles, but limit their exposure to mass and consumer culture by prohibiting radio and television. Both groups have a prescribed dress code for baptized women which contains common elements: a head covering and a modest, long, loose, simple dress cut in a church-mandated style worn uniformly by all women in the community (see Figures 2.1, 2.2 and 2.3). However, both groups have few restrictions on men's dress; these Mennonite men are indistinguishable from their non-Mennonite neighbors except on Sundays, where specific suits are worn.[3]

The groups' reactions to expulsion are different, however; while Eastern Pennsylvania Mennonites usually maintain some relationship, however strained, with family members who leave the church, Holdeman Mennonites practice shunning, a more severe form of social ostracism and social control, the threat of which is used to insure conformity.

The most conservative Mennonite and Amish groups are called 'Plain People,' a designation which immediately identifies the use of plain dress as one symbol of their conservatism. Plain groups use various cultural boundary markers to set them irrevocably apart from the wider society. Unlike the Amish, whose horse and buggy lifestyle is their primary symbolic device, the conservative Mennonite groups in this study rely primarily on dress – particularly women's dress (since men's clothing is much less regulated) – to mark their separation from the larger culture. Women's dress and behavior thus function as the pivot point on which turns the groups' distinctiveness, bearing as it does the entire weight of cultural separation for Holdeman and Eastern Pennsylvania Mennonites. As such, women's dress and behavior is subject to a high degree of social control, as we explore below.

Mennonite History and Beliefs

Ethnographic research requires the field worker to be totally conversant with and immersed in the belief and value system of the group under study prior to entering the field and collecting data. This is a rather unique culture and in order to understand the salience of dress as a cultural boundary marker, it is necessary to provide some background on the historic and religious history of America's Mennonites.

Small numbers of Mennonites first immigrated to Pennsylvania early in the eighteenth century in search of religious freedom; later immigrations to Pennsylvania during the nineteenth century and to Kansas and other Midwestern states during the nineteenth and twentieth centuries swelled their numbers (Arthur, 1992, 1997; Boynton, 1986; Hiebert, 1973). Today, more than a quarter of a million Mennonites live in the United States, among which the conservative communities are the fastest growing segment (Nolt, 1992). Their roots are in the Protestant Reformation of the sixteenth century, when their ancestors, a small, radical group known as Anabaptists, organized disciplined communities of believers who espoused a more literal interpretation of the New Testament. Anabaptists stressed lay leadership, nonviolence, the separation of church and state and adult baptism. Branded by society at large as heretics, Mennonites migrated from Germany and Switzerland to Holland and Russia to escape religious persecution. When they came to North America, Mennonites established isolated farming communities and sought to live simply and in peace (Boynton, 1986; Hiebert, 1973). Members practiced 'nonconformity,' that is, a belief in the value of separating themselves as much as possible from the ways of the world. Then as now, Mennonites based their belief in nonconformity on the Scripture verse from Rom. 12:2 (RSV), 'Do not be conformed to this world, but be transformed by the renewal of your mind, that you may prove what is the will of God, what is good and acceptable and perfect.' Sometimes known as a doctrine of 'separation from the world,' this belief continues to be pivotal.

Separation from the World

The traditional Mennonite practice of separation from the world links social control and clothing norms. Mennonites believe that there are two kingdoms – the Kingdom of God and the Kingdom of the world. Although located here in the physical world, Mennonites believe that they belong to the Kingdom of God, preferring to think of themselves as 'in the world, but not of it.'

Women in our study believed that the church's doctrines of separation from the world were responsible for helping them to live godly lives. Rebecca regarded the church teaching on separation as having 'protected me from ruining my life by having low [moral] standards or whatever.' Lydia credited the church with fostering her devotion to God: 'I see separation as a help to remind me who I serve.' In these ways conservative Mennonite women have internalized the value of cultural separation from the world.

Historically, separation from the world was easier to maintain when Mennonites were physically isolated in remote, rural communities. However, the population pressures of an expanding nation and the resulting impact of interaction with outsiders threatened Mennonite cultural cohesiveness. Conservative groups responded by codifying many of their old traditions, especially rigid codes of dress. Separation thus became more symbolic than physical, conveyed primarily by means of sartorial statement.

Throughout Mennonite history, the clothing adopted by Mennonites resembled the styles of the time, but was very plain (Gingerich, 1966). Even today, in the vocabulary of our informants, 'plain dress' is the generic term used to refer to the distinctive, old-fashioned, un-ornamented style of clothing worn by Amish and conservative Mennonites, sometimes called 'Plain People' for this manner of dress. Conservative Mennonites justify their distinctive dress by citing the Apostle Paul's instructions that women should adorn themselves in modest apparel, with sobriety, foregoing 'costly array' in favor of 'good works' (I Tim. 2:9,10). The Holdemans claim that this lack of emphasis on external beauty leads to the expression of spirituality (Scott, 1986).

One of the specific concerns of John Holdeman's reform movement of the 1850s was that Mennonites had begun to dress more like the external society, thus losing their religious distinctiveness. Following his break from the larger body of Mennonites, Holdeman insisted that his followers, known as Holdeman Mennonites wear clothing that indicated their conservatism and separation from the world at large. For women, this meant wearing a long dress with high neck and fitted waist (Hiebert, 1980). Today the prescribed dress code for Holdeman women is characterized by shirtwaist dresses with wide skirt and fitted bodice, buttoning down the center to the waist, generally worn with a small collar and belt.

In like manner the Eastern Pennsylvania Mennonite Church was founded in the mid-twentieth century in large part because conservatives feared the loss of plain dress for women (Graybill, 1998). Their prescribed dress code for women features a long-sleeved dress, styled with a cape over the bodice and little ornamentation (see Figure 2.3). For both groups, jewelry, cosmetics and the cutting of hair are prohibited, according to Biblical injunction.

Patriarchy and Social Control

Mennonite patriarchy has its roots in the Bible, the authoritative word of God. For conservative Mennonites, male power is a divinely ordained hierarchy of 'God, man, woman. That's God's chain of command,' as one informant put it.

The Mennonite women's head covering visibly expresses a woman's submission to male authority, both at home and in the church. Kristina, an

Figure 2.1. Holdeman Mennonite family at home. The father is wearing a plaid shirt and jeans, the mother is in orthodox dress, the teenaged daughter in fancier dress typical of unmarried women. Both wear headcoverings. The youngest daughter wears loose dress typically worn by girls prior to baptism. Illustration by Margaret McKea.

Figure 2.2. Orthodox women (left) dress according to a strict dress code based on Holdeman ideals. Marginal women (right) alter the normative pattern in numerous ways, resulting in dresses that are considered acceptable, although they deviate from the norm. Illustration by Mary Lou Carter.

Figure 3. While men are expected to wear a collarless suit jacket, known as a plain
suit, when attending church, women are required at all times to wear a
dress style with an extra layer of fabric, or cape, over the bodice. This
cape dress is always worn with the prescribed head covering, as shown.
Used by permission of the Pennsylvania German Society.

Eastern Pennsylvania Mennonite, described the head covering as 'a sign that
you acknowledge God's order of headship.' Or as Mary, a Holdeman Mennonite put it; 'Women wear a black head covering over uncut hair pinned into
a bun to symbolize the woman's submission to God and her husband.' In
this way the head covering represents a woman's ultimate acceptance of the
community's patriarchal social order.

In this divinely ordained hierarchy, all men exercise informal power, while some men – ministers, deacons and school board members representing some 20 percent of the male population in the Holdeman community – are in formal positions of power. Informally, women defer to men. Lydia described church business meetings in the Eastern Pennsylvania community where women 'are even allowed to voice our opinions, but basically, the men – they do most of the talking. . . . We *can* share our feelings, but the woman basically does not take authority over the man.' Formally, male ministers and bishops are charged with the task of maintaining social control through reproval and expulsion.

In fact, some scholars have disputed whether the lived reality of conservative Mennonite and Amish women is, in fact, as harsh as the patriarchy would suggest (Olshan and Schmidt, 1995). While a full discussion of this point is outside the scope of our paper, it should be noted that conservative Mennonite women wield a certain amount of domestic power in the home setting, controlling the household budget and disciplining children in the absence of the children's father. Overall in family life, however, husbands are the ultimate authority. It also should be noted, as Graybill's interviews substantiate, that conservative Mennonites are not immune to such problems as spousal abuse and incest.[4]

Finally, conservative Mennonites state that clothing, as all of life, has to be brought under the scrutiny of New Testament standards, but in reality only women face that scrutiny. Although clothing for Holdeman men has changed with the times, women's overall dress and adornment practices have stayed consistent with nineteenth century practices. There are no specific dress requirements for conservative Mennonite men in these two churches, other than dressing simply on weekdays and wearing suits to church. In this way the clothing of conservative women visibly sets them apart from society, while their men are easily able to pass in the wider world. Mennonite patriarchy thus supports a double standard in dress.

Social Control of the Inner Body

The individual body is controlled by norms of the social body. To provide order, social groups define what is considered normative in terms of sexuality, emotional expression and socially acceptable modes of self-presentation (Turner, 1984). By defining and describing social roles and the normative behaviors expected to accompany these gendered roles, cultures provide a blueprint for women's lives. Among conservative Mennonites, a woman's major role is to socialize children and to support her husband. As Alma emphasized, 'A woman graces a man's life. She is his helpmate and her life is to be dedicated to him.'

Through enculturation the individual internalizes group norms and employs personal self-control to achieve voluntary compliance with those norms. In this way, enculturation leads to social solidarity. The ideal member of a conservative Mennonite community needs little external social control in order to remain within societal norms. Self-monitoring, in many cases, replaces the need for external social control.

Dress is an integral part of the process by which Mennonite women demonstrate self-control. Modesty in women's attire is an important social norm. As Rachel stated: 'Some people say there's no religion in clothes. But when I'm in them there is.' Mennonite women control the inner body by adhering to their group's religiously-based standards of plain dress.

Among conservative Mennonites, girls begin to exercise personal control during adolescence. An Eastern Pennsylvania Mennonite girl begins wearing the cape dress, designed to mask her developing figure, when she 'begins filling out.' At the same time that she is learning to be modest in her dress and behavior, she is preparing to join the church (at age twelve to fifteen). Religiosity, the focal point of her life during this time period, thus goes hand in hand with self-regulation of the body.

The norms of the social body control the individual body in terms of emotional expression, as well. Women are expected to be humble, somber and calm. According to Rebecca, for a woman not to be properly submissive 'would be uppity or lacking in modesty or in the graces that are supposed to be associated with womanhood.' Rebecca then went on to describe her mother, clinically diagnosed as manic-depressive and remarked matter-of-factly that when her mother is most depressed, 'that's usually when people in church look at her as being the most ideal because she's quiet and she's submissive and all that a woman should be.' As this conversation illustrates, conservative Mennonite women function within a limited range of acceptable emotions in deference to social norms.

An interesting incident occurred near the end of Arthur's fieldwork. She took Sarah and two of her teenaged friends shopping in a nearby town. Being away from their parents and other Mennonites led to a radical change in the girls' behavior. Wearing typical plain dress and head coverings, the girls played 'dress-up' with some of the more radical clothing found in stores and made quite a scene in a lingerie department by being loud and boisterous. Clerks openly stared at the girls, who were not demure, quiet and unobtrusive as young Mennonite women normally behave. This example illustrates yet another way in which emotional restraint is expected to characterize the inner body, at least in the presence of other Mennonites.

Appetite Control: Knowledge

Conservative Mennonite groups traditionally oppose higher education as unnecessary and un-Christian. Most feel that it leads to loss of faith because of its emphasis on 'secularism and humanism' (Discipline, 13). Both Mennonite groups in this study operate their own parochial schools emphasizing a 'Bible-based curriculum' through the tenth grade. Higher education is only rarely acceptable and must be approved by the ministers.

Specifically as it relates to control of the body, Holdeman Mennonites consider an appetite for knowledge to inspire too much abstract thought and encourage dissent. Often, having knowledge is perceived by the Holdemans as a means of exhibiting pride. Arthur was told that she would have to give up being a college professor if she wanted to join the church, because intellectual stimulation was another 'lust of the flesh', meaning that it was aimed at self-fulfillment, rather than spiritual enlightenment.

Pursuit of knowledge can also be a problem for members, as Sarah found out. She was fascinated by science and wanted to become a doctor from the time she was a little girl until that goal was denied by the ministers. Being a doctor was in opposition to women's roles as defined by the community and required higher education. Many suggested she lower her aspirations and become a vocational nurse, but she was determined to be a doctor. At seventeen, Sarah decided to enroll in a junior college with a small outreach program near her home. Formal social control was brought to bear on her when she was publicly censured and ordered to withdraw from school. She was interrogated in a public hearing and asked if she was having mental problems or was lesbian. Consequently, she was labeled deviant for not abiding by the norms and kept under the watchful eye of the ministers for several years. The social control measures were effective. She withdrew from school, later married and now has several children.

Appetite Control: Sex

Sexual desire is the most overtly controlled of the body's appetites. Shilling (1993, p. 90) notes that 'the restraint of desire has traditionally been concerned with the regulation of sexuality by systems of patriarchal power'. Weber discusses the fact that sexuality threatens fundamentalist religions and must be repressed in order to keep people focused on salvation (Weber, 1964). The sexual relationship poses a threat toward the spiritual one, according to our informants. Ruth succinctly stated that sex is 'for reproduction, not recreation.' Among conservative Mennonites, sexual expression is kept under tight rein and is only allowed within the confines of marriage. Public displays of affection are discouraged; married people do not hug or kiss in public, not even at their own weddings (Scott, 1986). In the Holdeman community, the sexes are kept separate from adolescence on. Unmarried men and women are never alone together prior to marriage, so premarital pregnancy among church members is not a problem in the Holdeman community. Eastern Pennsylvania Mennonites are permitted to date without chaperons after age eighteen, but dating only once every two weeks on Sunday afternoons is the norm (Scott, 1996). In church, conservative Mennonites sit separately by gender, 'due to the contribution that mixed seating makes to the moral breakdown' (Discipline, p. 14).

Among conservative Mennonites, motherhood and adulthood are synonymous. While infertility is rare, adoption is common, including increasingly frequent bi-racial adoptions in the Eastern Pennsylvania Mennonite community. The occasional spinster generally marries a widower later in life and may have stepchildren. While birth control is discouraged, members practice methods of natural family planning to space children. Sexual behavior between spouses is regulated by the Church. An expelled Holdeman woman related that the church held classes, with men and women meeting separately, to discuss what was and was not acceptable, in terms of sexual expression. In sum, the classes made clear that the sexual act was to be accomplished quickly and efficiently, with no time wasted on foreplay. 'What the ministers want is to make sure that God takes precedence even over the marital bond', she stated. While both sexes are enjoined to control sexual urges, the ultimate responsibility is assigned to women. These examples illustrate how conservative Mennonites seek to control sexuality through social regulation and restraint.

Social Control of the External Body

Through intense scrutiny of rigid behavioral and dress norms, women's external bodies are controlled by Mennonite social bodies. As Turner (1984) noted, the external body is controlled in its representation, its ability to communicate information about identity. For conservative Mennonites, an individual's personal identity is subsumed by the group's identity and identity is most visibly expressed in dress. Loyalty to the group is evidenced by the wearing of a uniform type of attire (Joseph, 1986). Visually, uniform dress suppresses personal differences, muting the idiosyncrasies of individual appearance. Uniform dress testifies to group solidarity; as Kristina said with satisfaction, 'It expresses that we are one body.' Conservative Mennonite women's dress thus enables the group to exert social control over its members.

The wearing of traditional Mennonite dress indicates a woman's willingness to submit to the control of the church and its dictates. Appearance is considered to be the external manifestation of inner attitudes. Because objective evaluation of a person's commitment to the faith is impossible, symbolic forms of self-expression are closely monitored. Visual cues are analyzed for signs of conformity to group standards. In the Eastern Pennsylvania Mennonite community a woman who fails to dress properly will be reproved by the local ministry. The following violations were cited as examples: wearing loud colors or large print fabric patterns, putting a large collar on a dress, hemming a dress too short, putting extra trim or a wide ruffle on the sleeves and top stitching with contrasting thread. As Ellen reflected on the preceding examples,

> You know, it seems like such a small thing. But it's finally an expression of pride, or rebellion, that's really what it is. . . . We feel the loud colors and the big prints would actually encourage attention to ourselves, rather than having a meek and quiet spirit like the Bible talks about.

In these ways external symbolic measures of dress and appearance standards are used as a means of interpreting a woman's inner religious qualities.

Mennonites who stray from the social norms are considered deviant and subject to both internal and external social control. Deviance is a social construct. It is through a process of meaning-attachment that acts or individuals are defined and labeled as deviant. Howard Becker emphasized this process when he wrote, 'Social groups create deviance by making the rules whose infraction constitute deviance and by applying these rules to particular people and labeling them as outsiders' (Becker, 1963, p. 9). The distinction between insiders and outsiders is clearly drawn by conservative Mennonites. The ideal social order centers on the traditional, rural Christian family and such values as humility, male authority and spiritual devotion. Insiders are church members, while outsiders include everyone else, including expelled Mennonites. The outside world is viewed with pity, suspicion and moral disgust; it provides a common enemy against which conservative Mennonites can unite and reaffirm moral superiority.

Kai Erikson (1966) notes that the definition and treatment of deviance is used as a means of value clarification and socialization by societies. The resulting conflict accentuates the differences between what is and is not acceptable in projecting a particular social identity. Those in control use boundaries to determine marginality and, therefore, deviance. As we will explore below, control of deviance is an effective method of maintaining the social boundaries of a group. Similar to Erikson's analysis, Mennonite ministers, acting in consensus, determine where the deviance boundaries are drawn.

At issue is conformity to social norms that are rationalized by religious dogma. What conservative Mennonites consider signs of religiosity are, from the perspective of this work, signs of socio-religious conformity. At the top of this stratified system are orthodox members who conform to the norms, are thoroughly enculturated and considered highly religious. They dress modestly. Lower status is accorded to members who deviate from many of the norms and are considered less religious. These marginal members are often young women who have not sufficiently repressed their sexuality. As they learn to do so, young women become more enculturated and there is a corresponding decrease in external constraints imposed by the group.

By way of example, orthodox and marginal women are discussed below. When interviewed about control issues, women primarily spoke about clothing; these examples illustrate the social control of the external body and its representation in the Mennonite community.

Representation of Sexuality

According to Turner (1984, p. 114), the social control of the body turns out to be 'crucially about the control of female sexuality by men exercising patriarchal power.' For conservative Mennonites, the control of female sexuality begins during puberty. During childhood, girls wear simple knee-length dresses, essentially unregulated. Young girls may choose from a variety of designs and dress styles. At puberty, a girl's clothing goes through a dramatic transition, when she adapts the one dress style available to adult women. Judith explained:

> The pressure increases continually. There is almost no restriction on little kids clothing, but there's less choice as they get older so by the time they are in the youth group [age sixteen to marriage] there's a uniform. This is to control sexuality.

Her sister, Ruth, elaborated on this theme when she said, 'clothing shows sexual repression, because it has to change in adolescence; it has to become more standard before you can marry'.

At the same time, ambivalence is shown toward both sexuality and its repression by the culture. Girls start using clothing for sexual display to attract marriage partners at the same time that ministers are requiring them to repress their sexuality. Eastern Pennsylvania Mennonite mothers remember their daughters having gone through a time of testing church limits by experimenting with hairstyles and extra trim on dresses which the mothers understood as being related to sexual desirability during the dating years. Depending on fit, the dress required of conservative Mennonite women can either conceal or reveal the body contours. While older, orthodox women will wear the dress fitted loosely and Holdeman women wear girdles to control movement, young women do the opposite. Young women abide by the overall dress code, but use the snug fit of the garment to show off female sexuality during the few years that are available to find a husband. Young women design dresses with a number of additional details to draw attention to the bodice. As an expelled Holdeman woman stated:

> You want to be married at eighteen; if you're not married by twenty-one you're an old maid. . . . So you put more detail in your dresses and fit the bodice as tight as you can. One time a Mormon guy asked me why the Mennonite girls make dresses with four lines pointing at the breasts – the darts really *DO* call attention to the bust!

John, an expelled man, stated, 'Young women have to keep their sexuality under control, but still must be attractive to the guys and still meet the letter of the law'. They must achieve what Laws and Schwartz (1977, p. 43) term 'a carefully calibrated degree of display and concealment'.

Once a conservative Mennonite woman has 'caught a man, there's no need to put so much time into your wardrobe,' said Rosanna. Married women no longer wear trim on their dresses, according to Kristina. After the first pregnancy, said Leah, 'they *expect you to calm down* [her emphasis], to dress more plain.' The terrain between display and concealment thus alters after marriage and pregnancy. A woman must still take care, however, to monitor the effect of her sexuality on others to avoid being seen as deviant. Because rigid conformity is the norm for this sect, it does not take much to be labeled deviant.

> It's good to look sexy, but only for your husband. But if you have a body that looks sexually attractive to others, you'll get in trouble with everyone. Your best friends will warn you to dress more modestly and ministers will attack you verbally and will look for signs of sin. (Mary)

Ministers continually watch women for behaviors that vary from established norms. An individual's behavior is interpreted in light of the deviance label applied by the ministers. This may result in an unequal enforcement of the rules. A marginal woman, whose sister Jane was orthodox, recalled a visit from the ministers:

> I was 8 1/2 months pregnant and overweight and I had borrowed a maternity dress from my older sister Jane and I was sitting there and they were giving me the third degree – asking why I do this, or that and I was crying and they asked why couldn't I please my husband. And one of the ministers said, 'Just take for instance that dress you're wearing.' It was a decent [typically Mennonite] dress, but he said, 'That dress is loud – a woman like you wearing such a dress is offensive.'

Jane wore it many times after I did, and never was reproved for it. I was the only one who was. And it was because they saw me as a threat. . . . The ministers always kept their eyes on me . . . after the baby was born, they continued to watch me, but with lust in their eyes.

Jane was the plain daughter in the family, while her sister had a voluptuous body and beautiful hair, which became a curse. Because the standard by which women are judged is the effect of their sexuality on men (especially those in authority), ministers see no contradiction in determining what is and is not considered acceptable female attire and attitude. Jane explained why the ministers expelled her sister:

The ministers were afraid of her; she is so pretty and she wasn't willing to submit. They couldn't get anything on her, really, except for clothes, which was what they harped on, but we dressed alike and they never bothered me.

Representation of Religious Orthodoxy

When friends and ministers speak with a woman about her unwillingness or inability to repress her sexuality, informal social control measures are exerted on the inner body. Aware of these levels of scrutiny, most women exert personal social control over the inner body to repress their sexuality. Personal control is clearly manifest in the appearance of orthodox women. Emma is a minister's daughter, married to a minister and has ten children. As a role model, she diets and dresses plainly and wears dark, solid colored dresses with no detail other than the required belts, collars and buttons. Interestingly, Emma makes hand-worked buttonholes for the buttons (as many as twelve per dress) that require weeks to complete. Although few women do this, she states that it protects her from accusations of 'dressing fancy.' Hand-worked buttonholes evidence her commitment to conservative dress and to Christian living, while simultaneously expressing her religious orthodoxy and high-status social location.

Status among conservative Mennonites is determined in large part by religious orthodoxy and is reflected in clothing. While orthodox dress avoids confrontation and raises status, deviations in dress lower status and invite controversy. Signs of individuality are seen to signify rejection of group norms and values. In discussing the expulsion of her aunt from the Church, Anna remembered, 'it was so sudden. There were no signs that she was in trouble – no changes in her behavior. Even her clothing was the same. I'd have expected to see some changes, like her dresses getting fancy or something.' A minister's daughter who left the church at nineteen but still lives in Bend, concluded:

define and defend their boundaries and argued (1970) that the more value people give to social constraints, the more value they set on symbols of bodily control. In continuing Douglas's line of thought, Turner (1984 showed how individual bodies are constrained both internally and externally. He argued that the social control of female bodies is an essential task of patriarchies.

Much of the literature in the emerging field of the sociology of the body is theoretical; our ethnographic case studies substantiate both Douglas's and Turner's theories and shows the soundness of their theoretical base. Of significance in this research is the impact that men have in both the social control of women and the social definition of reality in conservative Mennonite life. Mennonite women were subject to much greater social control than Mennonite men and while many women internalized these elements as personal control, men defined the situations in which women were labeled deviant.

The social structure of conservative Mennonite groups requires a high degree of conscious control that is manifested in the social control of women's bodies, both internally and externally. Conservative Mennonites are acutely aware of the power of appearances to show integration of the various levels of the self; consequently, every aspect of a woman's external body – her social self, her sexual self – must manifest a symbolic acceptance of religious values. Religious dogma is used to rationalize a rigid dress code, since clothing is seen as evidence of either religious conformity or deviance. Because deviation from socio-religious norms is considered threatening to the sect as a whole, it must be controlled. The greater a woman's deviance from the dress code, the more likely it is that she will encounter formal and informal means of social control.

This research indicates an analytical need to go beyond narrowly drawn descriptions of deviance. Within the conservative Mennonite community, the importance of informal deviance labeling is apparent in the treatment of marginal women as a stigmatized group. Schur (1984) noted the recent focus on informal deviance-defining and suggested that the stigmatization of women be addressed through qualitative fieldwork. Our research supports this recommendation. Analysis of social control in studies such as our own should provide an opportunity to understand deviance and social control of the body in routine interaction, while concurrently shedding light on gender and power relations.

Finally, this case further substantiates Henley's (1977) conclusion that nonverbal interaction between men and women illustrate not simply sex differences, but power differences. Bodies are affected by power relations and enter into dialogue between individuals and their social groups over social definitions of the self. Further, this research shows how bodies can be used to legitimate social inequality. It is in the domain of control, gendered power differences and definitions of female deviance that we suggest further research is needed.

Notes

1. For the sake of anonymity, all names of people and places in this chapter are pseudonyms.

2. The formal name, 'Church of God in Christ, Mennonite', was rarely used; rather the formal designation was typically 'Holdeman Mennonites'. Informally, members usually refer to themselves as Holdemans, after their founder. They also refer to themselves in a more general sense as Mennonites.

3. Eastern Pennsylvania Mennonite men are expected to wear a collarless suit jacket called a plain suit to church on Sunday; during the week they dress in generic work clothes, which are not regulated by the church. Similarly, Holdeman Mennonite men wear simple suits to church on Sunday, but these suits are no different from those worn by their non-Mennonite neighbors, except that they are always dark and plain. On Sundays, long sleeved shirts are worn and are buttoned up to the neck. No ties are worn. Like the Eastern Pennsylvania Mennonite men, Holdeman men are indistinguishable from their neighbors on other days of the week and favor jeans and plaid or plain shirts.

4. More than anything else, the quality of a woman's relationship with her husband may mitigate the degree of patriarchal social control she experiences. Lois, a former member of the Eastern Pennsylvania Mennonites, described some marriages within the church as evidencing a mutual respect and equality surprising in light of the church's patriarchal rhetoric. But in other cases, she reflected, 'Some of the men use the church's interpretation as a license to express power and for some women that's everything from completely terrible to, you know, just sort of a pain that's constantly there.'

References

Arthur, L. B. (1992). Idealized images: Appearances and the construction of femininities in two exclusive organizations. (Doctoral dissertation, University of California, Davis, 1992). *Dissertation Abstracts International, 51,* 9302588.

Arthur, L. B. (1997). Clothing is a window to the soul: Social control in a Mennonite community. *Journal of Mennonite Studies, 15. 11–30.*

Becker, H.S. (1963). *Outsiders.* New York: Free Press.

Boynton, L. (1986). *The Plain People: An ethnography of the Holdeman Mennonites.* Salem, WI: Sheffield Publishing Co.

Discipline of the Eastern Pennsylvania Mennonite Church and Related Areas (1993) (Available from Eastern Pennsylvania Mennonite Church, sixth statement).

Douglas, M. (1970). *Body symbols*. Oxford: Blackstone.

Douglas, M. (1982). *Natural symbols*. New York: Pantheon Books.

Eicher, J. and Roach-Higgins, M. E. (1992). Definition and classification of dress. In R. Barnes and J. Eicher (Eds.) *Dress and Gender: Making and Meaning in Cultural Contexts*, New York: St. Martin's Press.

Erikson, K. (1966). *Wayward puritans: A study in the sociology of deviance*. New York: John Wiley.

Gingerich, M. (1966). Change and uniformity in Mennonite attire. *Mennonite Quarterly Review*, 40 (4): 243–59.

Goffman, E. (1971). *Relations in public*. New York: Harper and Row.

Graybill, B. (1998). Mennonite women and their bishops in the founding of the Eastern Pennsylvania Mennonite Church. *Mennonite Quarterly Review*, 72 (2). April, 251–273.

Henley, N. (1977). *Body politics: Power, sex and nonverbal communication*. Englewood Cliffs: Prentice-Hall.

Hiebert, C. (1973). *The Holdeman people*. Pasadena, William Carey Library.

Hostetler, J. (1996). Amish Society, 4th Ed. Baltimore and London: Johns Hopkins University Press.

Joseph, N. (1986). *Uniforms and non-uniforms*. Westport, CT: Greenwood.

Laws, J. and Schwartz, P. (1977). *Sexual scripts: The sexual construction of female*. Hinsdale, Il: Dryden Press.

Nolt, S. (1992). The Mennonite eclipse. *Festival Quarterly*. Summer. 8–12.

Olshan, M. and Schmidt, K. (1994). Amish women and the feminist conundrum. In D. Kraybill and M. Olshan, (Eds.), *The Amish Struggle with Modernity*. Hanover, NJ: University Press of New England, 215–229.

Poll, S. (1962). *The Hasidic community in Williamsburg*. New York: Glance Free Press.

Rubinstein, R. (1995). *Dress codes: Meanings and messages in American culture*. Boulder, San Francisco and Oxford: Westview Press.

Roach-Higgins, M. and Eicher, J. (1992). Dress and identity. *Clothing and Textiles Research Journal*, 10 (1), 1–8.

Schur, E. (1984). *Labeling women deviant: Gender, stigma and social control*. New York: Random.

Shilling, C. (1993). *The body and social theory*. London: Sage.

Scott, S. (1986). *Why do they dress that way?* Intercourse, PA: Good Books.

Scott, S. (1996). *An Introduction to Old Order and conservative Mennonite groups*. Intercourse, PA: Good Books.

Thompson, W. (1986). Deviant ideology: The case of the Old Order Amish. *Quarterly Journal of Ideology*, 10 (1). Jan. 29–33.

Turner, B. (1984). *Body and society*. Oxford: Basil Blackwell.

Weber, M. (1964). *Religion and society*. Boston: Beacon Press.

3

Sacred Dress, Public Worlds: Amish and Mormon Experience and Commitment

Jean A. Hamilton and Jana M. Hawley

The intimate relationship between the forms and meanings of dress and the world view of a cultural system in which it is manifested has been well established. In complex cultural systems, supernatural ideologies tend to become highly bureaucratized and evolve into what is currently recognized as *organized religion*. Such religions, besides professing a theology, also evolve a world view that embodies a perspective about the place of that group in the external world.

In *The Elementary Forms of Religious Life*, Durkheim (1915) articulated the distinction between *sacred* and *profane*. Since then, scholars who have been critical of Durkheim's assertion of sacred/profane as empirically discoverable social facts or as mutually exclusive categories (see Evans-Pritchard, 1968 and McDonald, 1986) have, nevertheless, asserted the usefulness of the sacred/profane distinction as a heuristic device. Firth's (1996) recent discussion of *the sacred* is especially relevant to this study in its attention to the sacred quality of particular material things and the sacred symbols they embody, rather than just the sacred quality of behaviors and beliefs. For Mormons and the Amish, both the form and function of items of everyday dress are *de rigueur* because of the religious beliefs and commitments of the wearers. These items, thus, take on the quality of the *sacred*.

This work explores the relationship between the sacred everyday dress and world views of two uniquely American religious groups, the Amish and the Mormons, the latter officially know as the Church of Jesus Christ of Latter Day Saints (LDS) and also commonly called Latter Day Saints. Of particular interest are the ways these two groups see themselves vis-a-vis the external, secular world. Both the Amish and Latter Day Saints are minority groups. Both have been persecuted throughout their histories, sometimes vigorously and both are still commonly misunderstood. Thus, for both groups, how they relate to the dominant society continues to be an important issue. The sacred everyday dress of both groups, which is intimate to their own conceptions of themselves as believers, both determines and facilitates how this articulation with the dominant society will occur.

Research Method

Discovering the richness of human behavioral and cognitive phenomena associated with the social construction of meaning calls for an inductive, qualitative approach to inquiry that is grounded in naturally occurring behavioral contexts. Such an approach also encourages the possibility of theoretical discovery. Specifically, the data reported in the chapter results from the research strategy of *participant observation*, common to cultural anthropological research.

While both researchers were involved in the gathering and analysis of data from both populations, each researcher took *primary* responsibility for one of the two groups. The Amish data were collected during an eleven-month period of participant observation in and around Schumok (a pseudonym), a town of about 560 in a Midwestern state. At the outset, Hawley worked without pay for the owners of an Amish grocery and dry-goods store. Thus, she became 'known' quickly as one who had the confidence of these important members of the Amish community. Her network of informants quickly widened, mostly as a result of her willingness to act as a taxi driver, to the extent of 50,000 miles during the research period, for Amish passengers who provided ready data and data checks on a variety of topics. Over time, the researcher became trusted and welcomed in a variety of Amish community activities. By the end of the research period, she had attended Amish meal-times, birthday parties, auctions, weddings, singings, volleyball games, work bees, hospital visits, shopping trips to surrounding towns, barn raisings and a host of more routine daily events.

Hamilton had the advantage of having grown up in an LDS home in which LDS theology and practices regarding sacred dress were part of her everyday experience. The challenge, then, was to discover in what ways the rules and behaviors regarding every day, sacred dress for Mormons may have changed over the thirty-year period of the researcher's relative detachment from Mormon life and culture. The researcher had maintained regular contact with many LDS friends and family members over these years. Thus, initial access was not a problem. Rather, the challenge was to ensure that assumptions, remembrances and understandings accumulated over the lifetime of the researcher were indeed timely, reliable and currently characteristic of a wider range of practicing Mormons than her personal experience suggested. To this end, the researcher conducted more than two dozen formal and informal conversational interviews with Mormons located both in Utah and a Mid-western state. Informants included local congregational leaders, extended family members and friends of Mormon friends and their family members.

Absence of Parallel Methods

Three differences between these two groups made it neither possible nor appropriate to approach this query in exactly the same way. First, Mormons do not live in isolated communities, nor do they attempt to exclude outsiders from their daily lives; thus, access to them is far easier initially than it is with the Amish. Second, there is no central Amish Church organization; they are not good record keepers and little reliable data in the way of books, letters, diaries and the like are available to outsiders. By contrast, Mormons are committed record keepers and the LDS Church organization maintains extensive archives and collects and publishes demographic data regularly in sources such as the *Ensign*, a monthly Church periodical. Third, the Amish wear their sacred dress on the *outside*; it is visible – recognizable from several hundred yards away. It hangs in full view on outdoor clothes lines on Amish farms and Amish women are normally at some stage of sewing something new when one visits them in their homes. Because Mormon sacred dress, however, is an *undergarment*, it is not visibly apparent except to the most intimate observers and Mormons are not recognizable to others as such by virtue of their wearing it. For the *outsider* researcher, therefore, virtually no observational data can be garnered on Mormon sacred dress.

Because sacred dress is *sacred*, we have attempted to be entirely respectful in investigating the topic with both groups and with what we have written in this chapter. When told there were fine details we should not ask about nor expect to uncover, we have left those areas alone.

Amish and Mormon Cultural Contexts

Amish History, Theology and Culture

The Amish are an outgrowth of the sixteenth-century Swiss Anabaptist movement, in turn a product of the Protestation Reformation. Like the Mennonites from whom they split in the seventeenth century, the Amish were persecuted relentlessly and came to view seclusion as a dominant survival strategy. The bulk of the Amish arrived in the United States in the early eighteenth century and settled initially in the area of Lancaster County, Pennsylvania along with their Mennonite neighbors. By the nineteenth century, disagreement regarding the issue of strict versus loose discipline resulted in small groups of Amish leaving and establishing new communities, first in Ohio in 1808 and later in other Midwestern states (Hostetler, 1980). Although many demographers and sociologists once expected the Amish to assimilate into the dominant American society, the Amish population in North America has doubled every twenty-two years since the beginning of the twentieth century (Hostetler, 1989). By 1990, it was estimated that over 165,000 Amish people were living in the North America (J. Hartman, personal communication, Spring, 1991) scattered among 750 congregations. Interestingly, no Amish congregations remain in Europe today (Hostetler, 1955).

Amish Theology. In addition to a strict Church discipline implemented through excommunication and the social avoidance of wayward members, including family members, Jacob Ammann, who broke from the Mennonites and founded the Amish religion, also favored a number of other principles grounded in particular scriptures. These principles included: (1) the authority of scriptures alone in matters of faith as well as action, (2) the rejection of violence in matters of faith as well as action (a position which eventually led to conscientious objection) and (3) the separation of the Amish from the dominant society in which they lived. Additionally, Ammann instituted ritual foot washing, biannual, rather than annual communion, the use of plain clothes and beards for adult men.

Clearly, particular scriptures shaped both Ammann's perspective and that of his followers. The Apostle Paul's admonition in his letters to the Romans, Romans 12:2, was seen as encouragement to reject worldliness in appearance and action when he said, 'Be not conformed to this world' (*Holy Bible*, 1948, p. 203). Further, Paul's writings to the Corinthians, in 2 Corinthians 6:14, were influential as counseled the followers of Christ, 'Be you not unequally yoked together with unbelievers: for what fellowship hath righteousness with unrighteousness? [*sic*] and what fellowship hath light with darkness?' (*Holy Bible*, 1948, p. 229). Additionally, the *Martyr's Mirror*, while not scripture *per se*, continues to hold a place of honor in most Amish homes. It contains chronicles, memorials and testimonies of the persecutions suffered by Amish forebearers, and serves as a constant reminder of the days of their most severe persecution.

Amish Culture. Fundamental to Amish culture is a commitment to family and community, a recognition and reliance on the authority of local Church leaders for regulating individual behavior and high value on individual humility (as opposed to pride), submission (rather than disobedience) and stewardship (rather than greed). Personal property is viewed as a gift from God and obligates one to responsible stewardship. Other Amish values include a strong work ethic, thrift, a reverence for longstanding tradition, a willingness to share resources with those who have more need and a commitment to an agricultural lifestyle. Each of these values is embedded in a structure that promotes community and family togetherness and opposes acquiescence to the dominant cultural system. Their work patterns become a ritual part of their daily lives; thus they view labor-saving technology as a threat to their cultural system (Kraybill, 1989).

Because there is no central Amish Church nor cultural bureaucracy from which local Amish groups get direction, rules are locally made and imposed by local Church lay leaders who are selected from within the local Church congregation. Although not always codified, the fundamental rules that operate within a community are contained within the *Ordnung*. The *Ordnung* details the way in which the Amish structure their daily lives – from whether or not community members may use diesel-powered milking machines, to whether or not women are allowed to refrain from wearing their traditional black stockings in the heat of summer. Across Amish communities, these rules range along a continuum from orthodox to progressive, or, as the Amish would say, from *lower* to *higher*. Low Churches are those that observe strict discipline, practice social avoidance and are the most technologically conservative. At the other end of the continuum are the high Churches that are generally more relaxed about all these areas. Despite the individual character of each Amish community, Anabaptist communities in general are very much in touch with each other. This is, in large part, because of the widely distributed *Budget*, an Amish/Mennonite weekly newspaper devoted to reporting the news from individual Amish and Mennonite communities all over North America.

Amish families are organized around traditional age/sex roles with power lying in the male gender and increasing with age. The Amish husband is responsible for the spiritual welfare of the household. Women are expected to carry out domestic chores, care for the young children and submit to the authority of the husband. Children are much wanted; they are perceived as an asset in Amish society. They provide labor on the family farm or in the family business and thereby perpetuate the Amish values of hard work and strong family ties. Except for a few areas in which they are unavailable, Amish children attend Amish schools through about the eighth grade. These schools emphasize basic skills, traditional Amish values and beliefs and community commitment (Hostetler & Huntington, 1989).

Mormon History, Theology and Culture

Mormons explain that they are not a splinter group of Catholics or Protestants. Rather, they claim that the true Church, which Christ had established during his ministry to the earth, had become corrupted and was lost from the earth shortly after Christ's death. Mormons cite Jesus' prediction (in John 9:4) when he said, 'I must work the works of him that sent me, while it is day: the night cometh, when no man can work' (*Holy Bible*, 1948, p. 129). Thus, Mormons believe that the true gospel of Christ was restored to the earth through Joseph Smith by divine revelation from God between 1820 and 1830. Like the Amish, early members of the LDS Church were severely persecuted and were chased around the Midwestern United States until, after Joseph Smith's martyrdom, Brigham Young led many Church followers to Utah in the late 1840s. After a number of confrontations with the Federal government, the Mormons found relative security in Utah (Allen & Leonard, 1976). Committed to proselytizing, the Mormon Church currently has a membership of just over 10,000,000 (Watson, 1998) with just over half that number in countries outside the US (Church membership, 1998).

Mormon Theology. Mormons' strong conviction of Christ's atonement dominates their belief system. They are genuinely dumbfounded when they are occasionally accused of not being Christians. To them, Jesus Christ is the center of their religion and his mission is described in both the *Bible* and the *Book of Mormon*, the latter of which they describe as a second witness to Christ's ministry. This additional understanding of Christ, combined with their convictions regarding the appropriate use of temples, sets Mormonism apart from other Christian religions.

As is the case with most other American established religions, Mormon church buildings serve as the locus for the weekly round of worship services and ancillary activities. Temples, by contrast, are viewed as more sacred than churches and have a special twofold function. First, they are a place where an individual may do his or her own *endowments*, certain covenants made with God regarding one's behavior and commitment. Children who are born to members of the Church are normally baptized on or shortly after their eighth birthday. Later on in life, they may go to the temple for their temple endowments. This ritual is seen as evidence of a more intense commitment to the beliefs members hold, one entered into at a more mature age and after more careful study of the gospel. Second, temples are the locus of rituals for oneself and one's ancestors, including baptisms and *sealings*, ceremonies in which families are sealed together for the eternities, a belief illustrated in the *Holy Bible* (1948) (see Genesis 25:8, Ecclesiastes 3:14, Malachi 4:6 and Matthew 18:18) and elaborated in Mormon scriptures. Thus, the belief that families can be united after death is a cornerstone of LDS faith. Because Mormons believe they are commanded to teach the gospel to the world and missionary efforts are increasingly successful in all parts of the world, the need for temples also increases.

Mormon Culture. Mormon culture and theology are closely linked. Among the religion's hallmarks is a commitment to family and the strengthening of family life, a commitment that is an outgrowth of the belief in the possibility of the eternal family. Mormons also exhibit a strong reliance on authority, a result in the belief that they are led by living prophets of God. Importantly, there are no paid Mormon clergy; rather, all offices in the Church are lay offices. Consequently, responsible Mormons expect to be active in their local congregations and have a strong sense of responsibility for the welfare and functioning of the entire congregation.

Like the Amish, Mormons place a high premium on personal moral responsibility, including honesty, chastity, fidelity in marriage and the establishment of family-centered homes in which to raise children. However, Church authorities acknowledged pressures on mothers to work outside the home and the increasing numbers of divorced parents in the Church. Church members are expected to refrain from tobacco, alcohol, tea and coffee. They are regularly encouraged to keep the Sabbath day holy by attending Church meetings, spending time with their families and studying the Scriptures. Church authorities encourage personal thrift and modesty in both dress and in lifestyle, but individual behavior is not monitored with nearly the same intensity it is among the Amish, due largely to the value Mormons place on individual agency.

The LDS Church is headquartered in a twenty-eight story office building in Salt Lake City, Utah. Locally, Church members are organized into congregations (wards), which combine to comprise larger membership units (stakes). Missionary work, something that has no role in an Amish community, is central to the culture of LDS families and to the Church's value system. Many parents save from the time their children are young to be able to send their children on missions for the Church. This generally occurs between the ages of nineteen and twenty-two and young people serve for eighteen months to two years. As a result of this commitment to proselytizing, the Church currently has 24,670 organized congregations in 143 nations and nineteen territories (First Presidency Letter, 1998).

Relevant Amish-Mormon Cultural Differences

LDS and Amish theology and culture are different in a number of ways, four of which are important to the ensuing discussion. First, since the establishment of their Church, Mormons have been enthusiastic supporters of the Constitution of the United States and seek to influence political life, rather than to separate from it as the Amish claim to do. While the Amish see government as a real or implied threat, Mormons believe that the early founders of this country were inspired by God to establish it as a place where the true Church of Christ could be re-established on the earth in safety.

Second, the Amish value only the most fundamental secular education, equivalent to about an eighth grade education and their schools spend much time teaching appropriate Amish values. By contrast, Mormons place a high value on both secular and spiritual education. The LDS Church encourages members to obtain as much secular education as is reasonable given their ability to do so. The Church owns and operates three universities, one of which, Brigham Young University in Provo, Utah, is the largest church-supported university in the United States. In addition, in communities where there are enough members of high school age to justify the expense, the Church operates a seminary program for LDS high school students in Church-owned facilities near the high school. Similar programs exist near many large university campuses around the country.

Third, while the Amish seek consciously to avoid the efficiencies that increased technological sophistication can provide, Mormons are committed to the use of modern technology to facilitate the Church's missions and agenda and Church members are as likely as their non-LDS friends and colleagues to be technological junkies. Moreover, the LDS Church relies heavily on sophisticated technology to facilitate genealogical record keeping and information transmittal, for running both the central and local Church bureaucracies and for facilitating the Church's overall programs.

Fourth and a combination of the first three, LDS culture is different from Amish culture in that while the Amish actively seek to avoid the external world – to be separate from it, while Mormons seek to be active in the external world and to influence it. In regard to their relationships with the world, the two cultures in this chapter are in opposition. LDS Church's enormous bureaucracy and its ancillary activities facilitate their integration into the larger society beyond the church. The latter include a motion picture production studio, television studios and satellite broadcasting facilities and publishing facilities that provide a variety of books, newspapers and multi-language periodicals including the monthly *Ensign*, which has served to provide documentary data for this chapter. The LDS's Church welfare program is in contrast to the Amish system of mutual aid. While the Amish system is extraordinarily efficient within and among Amish communities, the LDS Church's welfare program, with farms, canneries and storehouses around the United States, also cooperates with international relief agencies to provide food, clothing, shelter and medical supplies as needed throughout the world (Monson, 1998). These efforts, including the Church's commitment to missionary work, are also consistent with the theme that the LDS Church seeks to influence the world in which it exists, to draw attention to its theology and value system and to model these values in whatever ways possible throughout the world.

Amish and Mormon Sacred Dress

The data that follow result from the research process described earlier. It is worth noting that beliefs and practices of the Amish and the Mormons have been both romanticized and disparaged in the popular press over the past 150 years. In the following discussion, we have attempted to neither idealize nor discredit the beliefs and practices of both groups, practices that have historically resulted in contradictory data and misleading assumptions.

Amish Sacred Dress

Amish dress, like other aspects of their material world, is plain. It is also functional, economical to produce and relatively uniform among wearers who belong to the same community. From the time of Jacob Ammann, who advocated an outward appearance that would reflect the principle of humility over pride, the Amish have consistently appeared different to the non-Amish around them. The Amish in this study reported this same rationale, the elevation of humility over pride, for the form of their contemporary dress. The Amish dress that we refer to as *sacred* is the outwardly, observable dress that allows Amish people to be readily recognized as such without any additional identifying information. While some, including the Amish might argue that fashion is a foreign concept to the Amish, we disagree. One Amish mother who insisted that the women's dress in Schumok had not changed in her lifetime backtracked when asked if she could remember what her mother wore when she was a little girl. She could and indeed, skirts now were described as quite a bit shorter and bodices somewhat more fitted. Needless to say, while the rate of change (see Hamilton, 1990) is much slower than it is in the dominant culture and there are more limits on the character of the changes, Amish dress is clearly influenced by the dress of the dominant society.

Description of Amish sacred dress.   Women in different Amish communities make their dress from a range of different dress patterns or styles. In Schumok, the pattern dictates an open front bodice, elbow-length sleeves (or long sleeves in the wintertime) and a fitted bodice with a narrow band-style collar. The bodice is attached to a same-fabric belt of about two inches in width to which the dirndl type, center-front-opened skirt is attached with a wide lap. The bodice is held closed by straight pins inserted horizontally down the front to the bottom of the belt. The skirt always comes to just below the knee on young girls and unmarried women, but tends to be anywhere from two to six inches below the knee for married women, depending on their age. Colors vary, but those prescribed for married women in Schumok are quite dark in value and dull in intensity, in hues of burgundy, brown, navy blues and blacks. Unmarried girls are permitted to choose much lighter values of rose, greens and blues.

Around the house women are expected to wear the white organza prayer cap; outside the house, they are expected to don the traditional black bonnet over the cap. Women also wear sweaters and capes, always dark in color and they are expected to wear black hose and black shoes; however, unmarried girls and a few married women frequently go barefoot at home throughout the year. Amish women are expected to use no makeup.

Throughout the week Amish men are seen in Schumok in heavy denim and a commercially manufactured man's dress shirt with sleeve length depending on the season, leather braided suspenders, a felt or straw hat depending on the season and work boots. Amish adult men in Schumok wear full beards and no mustache. For Church, both men and women appear in dark dresses or suits.

Acquisition of Amish sacred dress.   Women in Schumok make most of the items of dress consumed by family members. These include women's and girls' dresses, men's work pants and men's suits and capes and winter coats for both sexes. A few items, such as women's bonnets, are custom-made by community specialists to whom community members often go to purchase specialty items. Other items are commonly purchased in 'English' (non-Amish) stores; these include shoes, hats, stockings, items of underwear and men's everyday work shirts.

Fabrics for women and girls' dresses, men's pants and suits and winter coats are normally purchased from one of three Amish dry goods stores in Schumok that stock appropriate fabric. Virtually all the fabrics purchased for making women's and girls' dresses in Schumok is a fairly lightweight 100 percent polyester knit, a fabric that would be impossible for the Amish to manufacture. This illustrates one way in which changes in Amish fashion are dependent on their willingness to embrace the technological advantages of the dominant culture they claim to reject. The polyester fabric had been readily embraced because it needs no ironing and dries quickly, on a line outside or in a basement.

Other items, including shoes, boots and underwear are generally purchased in a nearby market town about ten miles to the north of Schumok. During travel to other Amish communities, items are frequently purchased while traveling away from home on vacation, or to a wedding, an auction, or a family reunion. Traveling out of Schumok for a trip to Wal-Mart is something of an adventure and looked forward to with great anticipation. Women make virtually all the purchase decisions on such trips. The Amish are very resourceful in tailoring commercially available products to their own needs, buying, for example, black and white jogging shoes at Wal-Mart along with a can of black paint for painting the white running strip black.

While shopkeeping is an appropriate economic occupation for Amish entrepreneurs, they are generally expected to stock merchandise needed by Amish members of the community. To the extent that 'English' customers are willing to search out the location of such stores and purchase their products, they profit so much the more (see Hawley and Hamilton, 1996, for a complete discussion of Amish entrepreneurship).

Rules and stretching the limits. The rules of dress in an Amish community apply to visible dress and are enforced by the social coercion of the group. That the rules for Amish dress apply only to outwardly observable dress was first clarified when one of the authors, while baking pies with an Amish family, was asked to make a run to the basement for additional jars of peaches. There, along with various pieces of underwear drying on the line, were several pair of bright, colorful men's boxer shorts with Disney characters on them, clearly too commodious to fit anyone other than the only adult male living at home at that time. When asked about them later in private, the wife acknowledged that her husband wore them, that after all, nobody could see them and complain.

When one Amish mother and her daughter invited Hawley to go swimming with them to a quiet little pond at the back of the farm, she was baffled about what was considered appropriate to wear. Erring on the side of conservatism, Hawley showed up in cut-off jeans and a sleeveless T-shirt, while the two Amish women showed up in string bikinis. (Only women were present, which may have contributed to the garment choice.) Interestingly, this episode occurred shortly after Hawley had been seen wearing blue jeans by several Amish teenage girls in a nearby town. In Schumok, Hawley had always worn blue or khaki skirts with a white blouse, but by the time she returned to Schumok, the word had traveled to some of her closer Amish friends who expressed their relief to learn that the researcher was a normal English woman. They persuaded her to wear jeans thereafter.

As one might expect to find in any such community, Schumok not excepted, there is a handful of individuals who acted as self-appointed moral police. These people report what they believe to be behavioral infractions to the Church leadership with authority over the individual. If the leadership agrees, one of the male leaders will quietly discuss the matter with the person accused of stretching the limits too far. If the behavior is not corrected within a reasonable period, the two or three Church leaders will visit the individual again.

Interestingly, the failure of the Church leadership to take action when an alleged infringement is brought to his attention constitutes the mechanism by which change most often occurs in an Amish community. If the bishop ignores the accusation, the accuser will likely try to drum up support between his friends and neighbors and encourage them to put additional pressure on the bishop for action. Under such pressure, a bishop cannot easily refuse to take action. If the accuser fails in his or her efforts to garner support for his accusation, a new standard will have been initiated and will doubtless be adopted by others. In this way new ideas are brought to a head and are eventually voted on by the Church membership, possibly resulting in a change to the *Ordnung*.

For example, one Amish woman returned from a family reunion in Florida having purchased some dress fabric in a *higher* community there. The fabric was a rose tone-on-tone print. She enthusiastically made the dress according to the Schumok pattern and wore it one day to town. Several people commented to her that she must have just come from Florida, but their tone made it clear that their observation was also a judgment. She reported that she had decided not to wear the dress in Schumok again, thus avoiding the intercession of any Church authority. However, she decided to keep it as a traveling dress for the next time she made an out-of-town trip.

Minor infractions of the rules abound. Amish women, for example, are supposed to keep their hair covered except at home in the presence of close family members. However, when one Amish woman spent several days in the home of the researcher to be near a hospitalized relative, she routinely wore her long hair loose and uncovered while inside the house. As an additional example, while they permit unmarried women to use a bandanna to keep their hair covered while in public during the summertime, married women are supposed to wear the black bonnet in public, regardless of weather. Yet many married women were observed in town with only the white bonnet in the summertime. One woman noted that as long as the bishop's wife does it, she could also.

From the time a young person is considered to have come of age, between sixteen years and marriage, Amish children are given considerable license to run amok while their parents sigh and fret. This institutionalized practice, referred to as *rumspringa*, (meaning 'running around'), gives male children somewhat more license than female children and the period of license normally lasts longer for males than females, primarily because of the younger age of marriage for Amish females. While less so for males than females, this new-found freedom is commonly expressed for males through some experimentation with smoking, drinking and bar behavior. Some young Amish folks even leave the Amish community for a period to live English, while the family hopes the episode will be short-lived. Amish females are more likely than males to explore this liminal status in somewhat less egregious ways, but experimentation with dress is a common mode of expression.

To illustrate, about three months into the field work experience, the researcher was interrupted at her house in town at about nine o'clock one evening by three Amish girls ranging in age from seventeen to twenty. They wanted the researcher to drive them the thirty miles to a bar in a nearby market town. The young women were wearing makeup and were dressed in English, destination-appropriate dress. Only their Dutch accents would have given them away.

The instance of another young Amish woman illustrates the power of the community's judgment in matters of personal appearance and morality. She had reached an age at which, by Amish standards, she should have already joined the Church, but had not yet done so because she wasn't certain that she wanted to 'be Amish.' While this young woman dressed *Amish* when working at an Amish store, at other times, she usually dressed *English* and did little to hide this contradictory behavior. Church leaders felt she was setting a poor example for the younger employees and that her employers should dismiss her on this account. Eventually, the church leaders instructed the owners of the stores to fire the young women and they complied.

Mormon Sacred Dress

Fundamental to LDS culture and theology and fundamental to the LDS manifestation of sacred vestments, is the institution of sacred temples. Currently, the Church has fifty-one operating temples (twenty-three outside the US) and about twenty more in varying stages of planning and construction (Westwood, 1997). Mormons associate their *endowments* (the covenants made in temples) and the undergarment, (or *garment*, worn thereafter) with the symbolic connection between dress and faith. This was reported in Isaiah 61:10: 'I will greatly rejoice in the Lord, my soul shall be joyful in my God; for he hath clothed me with the garments of salvation, he hath covered me with the robe of righteousness' (*Holy Bible*, 1948, p. 831). During visits to a temple, members of the Mormon Church wear special white temple clothes. Outside the temple, however, what are referred to as one's *garments* are undergarments and are hidden by one's street clothes. Once endowed, a faithful Church member wears the *garment* for the rest of their life, as one would wear any undergarment.

Mormons explain that because they have no professional clergy, but rather subscribe to a system in which all faithful members of the Church share ecclesiastical responsibilities, the garment serves to remind the wearer of his or her special commitments. 'It is an outward expression of an inward covenant to the gospel principles of obedience, truth, life and discipleship in Christ,' and 'it symbolizes Christ-like attributes in one's mission in life' (Marshall, 1992, p. 534).

Garment description. For both men and women, the everyday *garment* is a one or two-piece bifurcated garment that covers the body from just above the knees to above the chest and upper part of the arm. There is some variation in neckline style and in the fullness of the legs. The design of the garment has changed over time. Both informants and secondary sources confirm these design changes. Joseph Smith initiated the existence of a temple garment about the time the Nauvoo (Illinois) temple was nearing completion in 1843. Then the garment consisted of unbleached muslin with sleeves to the wrists and legs to the ankles. In 1923, the Church authorized a new design that included sleeves to the elbows and legs to just below the knee (Buerger, 1994). Since then, minor design changes have been initiated, usually in consultation with LDS designers. While the one-piece garment is still available and commonly worn, since 1979, the Church has manufactured a two-piece garment which, according to informants, was accepted with enthusiasm.

Today, garments for both men and women are available one-and two-piece styles and are manufactured in a wide variety of fabrics and sizes. Regardless of style, the leg length is intended to come to the top of the knee. Women's garment tops are available in a rounded-neck and a sweetheart-neck style that generally correspond to bra line. Men's tops are also available in two different tee-shirt type necks. All garments have a sleeve, short for men and cap-style for women. Other undergarments such as bras are worn over the garment. Regardless of the style of garment selected, wearing the garment ensures that the wearers are modest in street dress as well.

Acquisition of the garment. Prior to the 1930s, there was no standardized garment *per se*. One elderly woman who lived in Virginia reported going to Salt Lake City in the mid-1920s for her endowments. Returning to Virginia, the woman visited her local department store where she purchased several *silhouettes*, an undergarment available for sale during that period; these she defined as her temple garments. She described the temple garment as a modest sleeveless, bifurcated one-piece undergarment, with wide legs coming nearly to the top of the knee and a bosom top with thin straps over the shoulder. This woman and other elderly informants who lived long distances from Salt Lake City indicated some pressure to substitute this for what at the time was commonly used in Utah and was more similar to a long legged union suit. The intent was to substitute something that would require fewer adjustments in street dress, rather than subject themselves and therefore their religion, to ridicule. Others recalled making their garments, which in those days were supposed to cover most of the arms and legs.

By the mid-1930s, the Church established a manufacturing plant, Beehive Clothing Mills, to produce garments to sell to endowed Church members. For women, the 'authorized pattern' consisted of a full-legged one-piece garment that came to just above the knee with a cap sleeve, designed so that regular street clothes of the time easily covered the garment. By the mid-1970s, the Church approved a two-piece garment style for both men and women. Today, the LDS Church continues to operate Beehive Clothing Mills, a manufacturer which produces garments for endowed Church members.

Garments are produced in a variety of authorized patterns in a variety of fabrics for both men and women. Prices of garments range from approximately $3.00 to $7.00, depending on the style and fabric. Church members assume these are sold at or near cost. The moderate prices would suggest the validity of these perceptions. One can purchase garments at distribution centers, usually located near temples throughout the world. In locales with a high Mormon population, retail distribution centers can be found in shopping mall settings as well. Beehive Clothing Mills also has an 800 number that members may use for placing mail orders.

Rules and stretching the limits.   Once endowed, members of the LDS Church are expected to wear their garments day and night for the rest of their lives. 'How the garment is worn is an outward expression of an inward commitment to follow the Savior' (First Presidency Letter, 1988). One is instructed about wearing the garment at the time of one's endowments. Interestingly, the absence of detailed instructions makes it possible for some to push what others feel are the limits regarding the rules for wearing them. 'The fundamental principle ought to be to wear the garment and not to find occasions to remove it. . . . Nor should [one remove] it to participate in recreational activities that can reasonably be done with the garment worn properly beneath regular clothing' (Asay, 1997). While the ambiguity in words like *reasonably* is troublesome to some, Church leaders have noted that 'how one wears the garment . . . is a measure of one's worthiness and devotion to the gospel' (Asay, 1997). Thus, the Mormon commitment to the principle of individual agency applies in this area as in others: 'This sacred covenant is between the member and the Lord. Members should be guided by the Holy Spirit to answer for themselves personal questions about wearing the garment' (First Presidency Letter, 1998). Indeed, endowed Church members may remove the garment for activities that reasonably require it, such as swimming. While there are no specific rules regarding swimsuit type, members are, in general encouraged to dress modestly. Thus, the appearance of a string bikini on an endowed woman at a swimming pool with both sexes in attendance would doubtless result in substantial clucking from others.

Informants expressed the belief that the garment represented the covenants they had made in the temple to live a certain way and that the garment had the power to protect them. One married woman in her mid-twenties explained, 'Well, it's never real clear what kind of protection they provide, but . . . if all else failed, just having your garments on would discourage you from getting too intimate with another man. . . [I mean,] how would you explain them to anyone else.' Other informants indicated that the garment could protect one from being tempted to do things one should not do, or from physical injury under certain circumstances. Still others indicated that a major reason for the garment was to encourage modesty. 'It's hard to run around half naked with your garments on,' explained one informant. Indeed, modesty is an important theme for Church authorities who encourage Church members to dress modestly. 'The principles of modesty and of keeping the body appropriately covered are implicit in the covenant and should govern the nature of all clothing worn. Endowed members of the Church wear the garment as a reminder of the sacred covenants they have made with the Lord and also as a protection against temptation and evil' (First Presidency Letter, 1998).

Still, it is not difficult to find examples of individuals who stretch the limits and of others who are judgmental about it. Informants were quick with stories of women who tuck the cap sleeve of the garment under their bra strap so they can wear sleeveless blouses or dresses, or of men who wear only their garment tops with biker shorts. The most frequently mentioned infraction concerned younger endowed adults who wear Bermuda shorts that fail to be quite long enough, which was judged by many to be not only as a breech of instruction for wearing the garments, but as the ultimate in tasteless appearance.

Not surprisingly, among the informants in this study, there was something of a split between older informants and younger ones, the older ones expressing more exasperation and disapproval with those who push the limits than younger endowed members did. Still, many younger endowed members expressed disapproval at compromising what they understand to be the expectations for wearing the garment. As one said, 'You know what the expectations are before you go [to the temple] in the first place. If you don't like them, then don't go till you do.'

Discussion

For both the Amish and Mormons, everyday sacred dress fulfills and reflects both micro and macro (Ritzer, 1991) objectives. The form and function of both Amish and LDS sacred dress are intimately related to the belief systems and ideological commitments held by both groups. While Mormons find the distinction of *sacred* appropriate for their dress, the Amish find the distinction a bit awkward, generally noting that they never think about it that way. 'It's just what we wear because we're Amish.' This is likely because Amish theological and community commitment is so intimately connected. With only a bit of probing, however, Amish informants easily acknowledge that they ground their distinctive dress in their religious ideology.

At the micro-level, one's sacred dress serves as a constant symbolic reminder to the wearer of personal spiritual commitments he or she has made and as a reminder of social identification (church organization/community). Thus, it is not enough merely to note the existence of the *form* of everyday sacred dress represented by these two religious groups. Members of other Western Christian religions use accessories to suggest messages of affiliation or commitment, e.g. head coverings or jewelry. However, the Amish and Mormons are unique in that faithful adult members literally *clothe* themselves daily in items of apparel that represent their spiritual commitment and organizational affiliation as they engage each day in the external world.

That their sacred dress serves, to members of both groups, as a *daily* reminder of commitments made cannot be over-stressed. In addition to the daily act of dressing and undressing, one's clothing requires time and energy in its acquisition and maintenance. Thus, we assert, one *chooses* it each day, an act of volition that requires one to reflect at some level on ideological commitments made, however rote and fleeting the reflection may be. Interestingly, members of both groups reported feeling 'naked,' 'undressed,' and uncomfortable functioning in the public world without sacred dress. Even those willing to push the limits and break the rules reported being uncomfortable in so doing.

Failure to *choose* sacred dress – pushing the limits too far or too often – when discovered by others, represents a breach of expectations regarding commitment that alarms community, congregations, family members and associates. With the Amish, such breaches are obvious to fellow community members. In such instances it would not be unusual to receive a visit from an Amish Church leader who would report the rumor and expect an explanation. Among Mormons, by contrast, while individuals are encouraged and expected to obey Church teachings, an individual's behavior regarding dress is not scrutinized to the same extent. In fact, the Mormon commitment to individual agency and the fact that Mormon sacred dress is an undergarment, discourages such intensive daily scrutiny, both in practice and in principle. Mormons are fond of quoting Church founder Joseph Smith, who said 'I teach [my people] correct principles and they govern themselves' (cited in Widtsoe, 1939).

While the principle of individual agency is an important doctrine for Mormons, social expectations and group coercion are powerful tools in regulating behavior, although not as much as they are for the Amish. While generalized encouragement and frequent general appeals to individual responsibility are means of encouraging adherence to the rules for Mormons, these modes of encouragement also protect the principle of agency. For the Amish, by contrast, *tattletale* enforcement is an efficient and direct way to correct an individual's inappropriate behavior. Interestingly, pushing the rules in an Amish community is a legitimate way to encourage change. Others are likely to imitate practices that are not nipped in the bud; left unchecked, such practices will eventually become the new standard. Thus as a guard against such changes, pushing the limits too far is generally nipped early and publicly.

The principle of individual agency, whether explicitly espoused or not, ensures that some individuals will push the limits in ways considered inappropriate. For Mormons, this is expressed via the examples cited above. Other infringements are associated with removing the garment to go swimming, which is permissible, but then lounging around the beach for the rest of the day in one's swimsuit, which some informants affirmed was explicitly discouraged. Similarly, one woman spoke critically of her brother who, she said, wore his garment tops without fail, but often left off the garment bottoms all day, explaining that he couldn't wear the garment bottoms with his biker shorts. The sister was frustrated that he seemed unwilling to acknowledge that wearing biker shorts was an inappropriate choice in the first place.

Both macro-level and micro-level differences in the sacred dress of both groups are completely consistent with the organizational goals and managerial structures of both groups. The Mormon Church is a complex bureaucratic structure with a Church headquarters that communicates efficiently and often with local congregations. Thus, the Church's concerns are made known easily through the Church's administrative structure on the one hand and through the communications organs of the Church, such as the monthly *Ensign* magazine, on the other. These expectations are also communicated informally among family and endowed friends.

Because of the Mormon commitment to agency and because Mormon sacred dress is an undergarment, the line between what is all right or not all right seems to some extent blurred. By contrast, the line is rarely blurred for the Amish. When Hawley provided a ride for an Amish male to a courthouse in a city nearly 200 miles from his home, he first removed his hat once well away from his community, then later his suspenders, neither of which he is permitted to be seen without in public. He commented that he believed he could then blend in better, noting that without his suspenders and hat, observers rarely noticed the funny way his trousers fastened. Interestingly, he failed to recognize that the cut of his quite distinctively Amish beard and lack of mustache would have identified him immediately as Amish to most rural people in that state.

At a more individual level, the sacred dress of both groups provides, or is believed to provide, a kind of protection to the wearer. This is an explicit point of doctrine for Mormons (Asay, 1997) and was commonly mentioned by informants. Exactly what sort of protection the garment provides, however, is not clear. While virtually all the LDS informants expressed the belief that the garment provided spiritual protection and encouraged them to keep the covenants they had made, some asserted that the garment also provided a physical protection while others seemed less certain of any *physical* aspect to protection. Most of the Mormon informants showed that they would feel vulnerable without wearing them, something that they must negotiate, for example, when going to the doctor or during hospitalizations.

The Amish, by contrast, suggested no supernatural advantage through wearing their unique dress. Rather, expectations from childhood and the rules of the *Ordnung* make their unique dress *de rigueur* for baptized Amish adults. Yet in a literal sense, Amish dress provides a very real protection from that which they fear most – contamination from the outside world. Their dress announces who they are and suggests that outsiders maintain social distance. In that sense, it works to keep them separate from the world and to protect them from worldly influences.

Finally, macro-level ideological goals of Mormons and the Amish are perfectly suited to the requirements of the every day sacred dress of these two groups. A garment-wearing Mormon is not obvious to an observer. Hidden by street clothes, the benefits of wearing one's garments, from the view of most members, are spiritual. However, as an unseen undergarment, they also facilitate the individual's immersion in and influence on, the dominant social world. This is consistent with LDS institutional goals. Mormons are proselytizing people. They wish to convert others to their religion and are successful in doing so, converting nearly 318,000 people in 1997 (Watson, 1998). Moreover, they wish to have influence in the world and over the social agendas of the dominant world. Garment-wearing Mormons include people across all social classes. The LDS Church's emphasis on education for its members positions them for activity in most professions and occupations, an achievement that would be difficult if they looked funny, unapproachable, or strange.

That the Amish appear unique, unapproachable and strange to most casual observers in fact facilitates their public goals as well. As people who seek to minimize contamination from the outside world and to maintain a commitment to a low-technology agricultural existence, their dress serves those ends. By any assessment, Mormons have more interaction with the public world, are more secular regarding daily concerns and activities and use virtually *invisible* dress symbols that facilitate their secular participation with the public world. This, in turn, facilitates their ability to influence it. The Amish, with no interest in influencing the external world, intentionally use *visible* dress as a boundary maintenance mechanism.

For Mormons, the commitment that governs the practices associated with their sacred dress is largely a function of the commitment to one's personal vows made in the temple at the time of one's personal endowments. For the Amish, the commitment that governs practices associated with their sacred dress is largely a function of the commitment one has to the one's social group. For members of both groups, the extent to which they transgress the rules regarding their sacred dress is largely a matter of the degree of commitment they have to the agreements, explicit and implicit, that they have made. For both, differences in rigor regarding the rules of dress are related to an individual's relative devoutness and commitment.

The sacred dress of both groups restrain one's behavior in the social world to some extent, albeit in different ways. At the same time it mediates the character of interaction that occurs with that world. Certainly individuals in both groups care what non-members think and for both groups, one reason for maintaining the standards of the group regarding their dress is to serve as an example to the world. Thus, however different the Amish and Mormons may be regarding their social and ideological agenda, their sacred dress serves to preserve their worldviews at the same as it mediates being both *in* and *of* the public world.

References

Allen, J. B. & Leonard, G. M. (1976). *The Story of the Latter Day Saints*. Salt Lake City: Deseret Books.

Asay, C. E. (1997, August). The temple garment. *Ensign*, 19–23.

Buerger, D. J. (1994). *The mysteries of Godliness: A history of Mormon temple worship*. San Francisco: Smith Research Associates.

Church membership reaches 10 Million (1998, January). *Ensign*, 74.

Durkheim, E. (1915) *The elementary forms of religious life*. Translated from the French by Joseph Ward Swain. New York: Macmillan.

Evans-Pritchard, E. E. (1968). *Theories of primitive religion*. Oxford: Clarendon Press.

Firth, R. (1996). *Religion: A Humanist Perspective*. New York: Routledge.

Hamilton, J. A. (1990). 'The silkworms of the East must be pillaged': The cultural foundations of mass fashion. *Clothing and Textiles Research Journal*, 8 (4), 40–48.

Hawley, J. M. and Hamilton, J. A. (1996). 'Retail entrepreneurial values in a bi-cultural community: Contentions and negotiations.' *Journal of Socio-Economics*, 26 (6), 639–61.

Holy Bible (1948). London: Collins Clear-Type Press. (King James Version.)

Hostetler, J. A. (1955). Old world extinction and new world survival of the Amish. *Rural Sociology*, 20, 212–19.

Hostetler, J. A. (1980). *Amish Society*. Baltimore: The Johns Hopkins University Press.

Hostetler, J. A. (1989). *Amish Roots*. Baltimore: The Johns Hopkins University Press.

Hostetler, J. A. & Huntington, G. E. (1989). *Children in Amish society: Socialization and community*. Baltimore: The Johns Hopkins University Press.

Kraybill, D. B. (1989). *The riddle of Amish culture*. Baltimore: The Johns Hopkins University Press.

Marshall, E. T. (1992). Garments. In D. H. Ludlow, (Ed.), *The Encyclopedia of Mormonism*. (Vol.2) New York: Macmillan.

McDonald, H. (1986). *The normative basis of Culture: A philosophical inquiry*. Baton Rouge, LA: Louisiana State University.

Monson, T. S. (1998, June). Our brother's keeper. *Ensign*, pp. 32–9.

Ritzer, G. (1991). *Metatheorizing in sociology*. Lexington, MA: D.C. Heath and Co.

Watson, F. M. (1998, May). Statistical report, 1997. *Ensign*, 22.

Westwood, B. (1997, June). Houses of the Lord. *Ensign*, 9–17.

Widtsoe, J. A. (1939). Priesthood and church government. Salt Lake City, UT: Deseret Book Company.

4

The Polynesian Cultural Center and the Mormon Image of the Body: Images of Paradise on Laie, Hawai'i

Frank Salamone

In his Forward to Richard M. Swiderski's (1986) *Voices*, a study of an Italian-American festival, Frank Manning (1986, pp. vii–viii) notes that the study of cultural performance not only blurs genres, as Clifford Geertz (1980) pointed out, it attunes the analyst to the multiple messages contained in the performance. These messages are innately dissonant and it is the task of the performance to seek to achieve harmony from its disparate components. That harmony, however, is often achieved through an ironic commentary within the performance itself that subverts its ostensible meaning.

The Polynesian Cultural Center (PCC) offers an excellent sphere in which to study cultural performance that contains a number of meanings, many apparently contradictory and even antagonistic. These messages are harmonized into a coherent message not necessarily one advocated by its sponsor, The Church of Jesus Christ of Latter Day Saints (Mormons) at Brigham Young University-Hawai'i (BYU-Hawai'i is an offshoot of the Church's main campus in Utah, Brigham Young University). Specifically, I will focus on aspects of presentation of the body in performance, following the general lead of Mary Douglas (1966, p. 15). The body is a model that can stand for any bounded system. Its boundaries can represent any boundaries that are threatened or precarious. The body is a complex structure. The functions of its different parts and their relation afford a source of symbols for other complex structures.

Douglas notes that there is often tension between the body of the self and that of society, by which she means one's personal and social identity. Douglas appears to be addressing the issue of achieved and ascribed identities, or at least aspects of symbol systems that have applications to this issue. She states (1973, p. 93)

> The social body constrains the way the physical body is perceived. The physical experience of the body, always modified by the social categories through which it is known, sustains a particular view of society.

From this tension emerges the possibility of elaboration and subversion of meaning systems. The very ambiguity within the structure that produces tension demands the release that play alone can provide. It is in playing with the system that creativity originates and freedom is possible, even while actors appear to accept the rules imposed by those in control.

The Project

I have long been interested in identity and its construction and presentation. That interest has led me to study religious conversion, ethnic change, gender roles and, more recently, tourism and its cultural presentations. Upon first reluctantly visiting the Polynesian Cultural Center in 1993 on a family vacation to Hawai'i, I was taken by the manner in which the Mormons had combined their religious program with a tourist center alleging to represent authentic Polynesian Culture. While engaged in an NEH (National Endowment for the Humanities) seminar on religion at Princeton in the summer of 1994, I discussed this notion with a faculty member from Brigham Young University in Utah. I had developed the idea to include the manner in which the PCC transmitted a version of Polynesian culture to its students and enabled those students to interact with tribal elders in a manner different from the normal course of such interactions.

Eventually, I received a small grant from Iona College to extend a conference trip to Hawai'i for one month in order to conduct a preliminary study of the PCC in January 1996. Through various Mormon acquaintances I contacted Max Stanton, a Mormon and an anthropologist, who aided my study, opened many doors and proved a fine friend. I spent my time at the PCC and BYU-Hawai'i visiting the PCC frequently, speaking with students and elders, filming and attending shows. Additionally, thanks to Greg Gubler, I was able to make extended use of BYU-Hawaii's archives. I was basically interested in the role religion played in the center, conflicts between various conceptions of 'authentic,' compromises in presentation, conceptions of 'modesty' and its relationship to religion and the role of the body in expressing culture. In turn, each of these questions was related to my life-long concern with identity and its construction and presentation (Stanton 1996, personal

Figure 4.1. Entrance to Polynesian Cultural Center. Photograph by F. Salamone.

communication; Gubler 1996, personal communication; field interviews at the PCC 1993 and 1996).

Origin of the Polynesian Cultural Center

The Polynesian Cultural Center (PCC) is often described by local inhabitants as Disneyland, Hawai'i. It is a multicultural theme park operated by the Mormon Church, located on the North Shore of Oahu in Laie, Hawai'i. The tourist is immediately drawn in by the festive nature of the setting and the various flags and decorations that signal a 'day off' with, perhaps, a chance to combine fun with cultural learning through tourism.

The PCC is laid out around a lagoon, made famous in Elvis Presley's movie 'Blue Hawai'i.' The tourist walks along the paths that traverse the lagoon, encountering seven Polynesian 'islands' along the way. These island cultures are spread throughout the forty-two acre site and represent Samoa, New Zealand (Aotearon), Fiji, Hawai'i, Tahiti, the Marquesas and Tonga. Additionally, the tourist can visit the Gateway Restaurant and dine with up to 1000 other visitors, see the canoe pageant show entitled the 'Ancient Legends of Polynesia', see the Night Show, or fit in a visit to the Mormon Temple (Fact Sheet, Polynesian Culture Center). The setting struck me as truly beautiful and the Polynesians were friendly and willing to answer serious questions. After an initial suspicious reaction from some performers, there was an openness that delights the typical anthropologist.

A series of events led to the founding of the Polynesian Cultural Center. In 1865 Mormons bought 6000 acres of land around the Laie area of Oahu's northern shore. Despite economic problems, Mormons remained in Laie and established a temple in 1919. The temple served as a magnet for Polynesian Mormons. Rebuilding of the Mormon chapel which burned in 1940 was delayed by the Second World War.

In 1940, however, the community imitated a long tradition and staged a tourist *hukilau,* which is a Hawaiian tradition of pulling in of fishing nets. The nets use pandanas leafs as floats and the term '*hukilau*' means 'to pull in the leafs.' A number of *hukilau* were held before the start of the Second World War. In fact, the first one was so successful that there was a *hukilau* every month on Saturdays in non-summer months. In the summer, there were two *hukilau* per month, continuing until 1971.

Various elements that became part of the Night Show developed as part of the stage show. Eventually, the seven island groups represented at the PCC participated in the *hukilau.* The knife dance, fire dance, various song-stories and hulas were first presented at the *hukilau* and the *hukilau* overlapped with the PCC from 1963 to 1971.

A final necessary condition for the PCC came about in 1955, when David McKay, President of the Church established a college in Laie. He said that viewing a flag raising ceremony at a Mormon school in Laie gave him the idea to celebrate the unification of cultures he saw in that ritual. McKay was well aware that a college founded for Polynesians would require money so that Polynesians could afford to attend. The success of the hukilau, especially its big show, provided him with an idea of how he could unite and preserve those cultures, or at least his version of them, while aiding Polynesian students to earn money for their education. This desire to merge the cultures was joined with the *hukilau.*

The *Hukilau* Festival of January 31, 1948, was held to raise a third of the cost of a new chapel, $12,000. Kawahigashi presented a plan to present a *hukilau,* similar to the ones that had aided the community in the late 1930s. Kawahigashi's (1968) description of the *hukilau* and the manner in which she organized it is an intriguing tale. She overcame numerous obstacles and received important aid from the Visitors Bureau. Combining *hukilau* song and native costumes was a stroke of good fortune that aided future hukilau. In 1952 the *hukilau* expanded beyond Hawaiian and Samoan presentations. Samoan presentations had been an addition to the original Hawaiian ones. They tended to be more 'spectacular' in their presentations, living up to the Samoan reputation as the happy people of the islands. According to Siufanua

(1990), Maori and Tongan dances were added to the show in a fortuitous manner. Two Polynesian students had brought back some Maori dances they had learned in Provo, Utah and added them to the *hukilau*. The Tongan section resulted from the fact that two Tongan girls were living with a Mormon woman in Laie and volunteered to be in the show.

There were a number of reasons for the demise of the *hukilau*. First, he growth of Laie's population and division into three wards; second, the subsequent end of the monthly preparations and the beginning of the quarterly *hukilau* cycle; and finally, the demand of Waikiki hotels for the same 20 percent commission on tickets they sold as other attractions, including the Polynesian Cultural Center; and the competition from Waikiki *luau*. The major competition, however, came from the Polynesian Cultural Center itself.

The Polynesian Cultural Center and Its Mission

There were three major reasons for founding the Polynesian Cultural Center: to preserve the culture of the Polynesian peoples, to provide employment and work through scholarships for the students attending the Church College of Hawai'i (now Brigham Young University-Hawai'i) and to provide direct financial aid for the Church College. A fourth reason, clear to any visitor, was added; namely, 'to provide a positive experience in introducing the Church of Jesus Christ of Latter Day Saints to the patrons of the Center.' Additionally, the first goal has been modified from preserving the culture of the Polynesian peoples to that of promoting 'selected aspects of the Polynesian culture and heritage which are in harmony with the doctrines and practices of the LDS Church.' (Stanton, 1977, p. 229).

The goal of the center, then, can be summed up as portraying an authentic view of Polynesian culture while benefitting students through allowing them to complete their educations, visitors through adding love to their lives and the Mormons through spreading their message. Such a bald statement of the situation leads one to ask the disturbing question of whose version of authenticity is being presented at the Polynesian Cultural Center. More disturbing, of course, is the question of what, indeed, is authenticity, for what is at stake here is conflict over just what is 'authentic' Polynesian culture.

The issues are complex and have troubled the Polynesian Cultural Center (PCC) from its earliest days. They bear on the type of ritualized presentations found at the Center, including the manner in which the ritualized body is presented. Ferre (1988, p. 3) states that there is an innate conflict between being authentic and profitable. Ferre quotes William Cravens statement (1978, p. A3) to the effect that a truly cultural performance would be quite boring and that it needs to be 'entertaining 'to keep it interesting. Ferre quotes

McGrevy as stating that there are three ways of defining 'cultural authenticity.' The first stresses an idealized past; the second way presents present day reality. The third presents an idealized future image of the culture (Ferre, 1988, p. 5).

Current Attitudes and Problems

Many people who have taken part in both the *hukilau* and the Night Show at the Polynesian Cultural Center, preferred the *hukilau*. They relate, in confidence, that the Night Show has become too commercialized and set to the tourists' tastes in performance and dress. There was more community involvement in the *hukilau,* they assert and consequently more authenticity. As one older women whose service stretches back many years told me, there is a feeling that the businessmen have taken over and are taking the heart out of the Center.

Stanton admits that many residents of Laie were not happy with the idea of the coming of the Center, fearing that it would ruin Laie as Waikiki has been ruined. Stanton (1977) and in personal conversations in 1996, recognizes problems regarding the 'authenticity' of the Center. He notes a 1973 workshop in which experts came from the island nations to offer aid in making the Center more authentic. He quotes with good humor the statement Bengt Danielsson made regarding the Tahitian exhibit as an example of 'anthropological science fiction' (Stanton, 1977, p. 230).

From a business perspective, the entertainment value of the Center is paramount, for if the tourists are not pleased then profits fall. When social scientists point out patent inaccuracies, they are met with a 'So what?' from businessmen. The dispute, however, cannot become too vocal on the part of the professors, for tenure depends on being a member of the temple and having good recommendations from other Mormons. Businessmen are quite influential in the governance of the Temple. Students, also, are virtually all Mormons and many depend upon working in the Center to pay their expenses.

The presence of one tribal elder for every seven youths does provide some stability and ensures some level of authenticity. Speaking with the elders does, in fact, reveal that they assume their responsibility with some seriousness and also that there is friction between them and the businessmen regarding the issue of authenticity. Elders dispute the need to water down the presentation of dances and other events and stress that the entertainment already provides an opportunity for instruction and could be structured to provide more. Certainly, elders were willing to speak at length with any who asked and to demonstrate traditional crafts, discuss the adjustment of their peoples to modern life and laugh at the disparity between their real 'native' costumes and the manner in which they have been adapted at the Center.

Traditional Dress

Traditional dress in Polynesia varies from island to island. In general, however, prior to Western contact, it was usually composed of only a lower body covering; loin cloths for males and wraparound skirts for females. Both sexes exposed their upper bodies. Throughout Polynesia the lower body was covered with skirts made either of leaves or a cloth termed '*tapa*,' (*kapa* in Hawai'i) made of shredded bark fibers pressed into sheets of fabric (Arthur, 1998).

Although specific clothing differed from island to island, a brief survey will suffice to present the general picture. Prior to Western missionary contact, Polynesians made their clothes, belts, bags and other accessories from the fiber of Pandanus leaves and Paper Mullberry trees. The use of floral garlands, termed *leis* for offering to the gods and sarongs, called *lavalava* in Samoa, were found throughout Polynesia.

Prior to missionary contact, Hawaiians covered their lower bodies with barkcloth (*kapa*) garments referred to as *malo* (a loincloth) for men and *pau* (a skirt) for women. Chiefs wore feathered cloaks and head-dresses fashioned from red and yellow feathers. Missionary women, unhappy about the exposure of female breasts, gave Hawaiian women chemises (slips) to wear, which were named *muumuu* by the Hawaiian women. The Missionary wives also invented a form of dress, termed the *holoku* to be worn over the *muumuu*. The *holoku* was a long, loose dress without a waistline, introduced in 1820. By the mid nineteenth Century, the *holoku* had become standard dress for Hawaiian women and western dress had become typical clothing for Hawaiian men (Arthur, 1997). The *holoku* became a likely model for the loose gowns that later came to be known as Mother Hubbards and were worn throughout the Polynesian islands after missionary contact (Arthur, 1998). Christian missionaries, including Mormons, have been satirized for their imposition of Mother Hubbards and similar dresses.

Missionaries also influenced clothing changes in Tonga, Fiji and Tahiti. Traditionally, dress on these islands was similar to that found elsewhere in Polynesia. Tongan *tapa*, however, has it own peculiar characteristics. It is decorated by tracing a relief pattern that is under the cloth after which the traced lines are painted. In contrast, *masi kesa*, Fijian *tapa*, is noted for its geometric patterns. These are made with stencils constructed from a mixture of green pandanus and banana leaves. Fijians add red coloring made from a combination of clay and a black pigment obtained from the candlenut, a nut whose oil was placed in lamps (Kennett, 1994).

Tahitians called their wraparound robe a *pareu*. They hand blocked or painted these robes in bright colors. Missionaries changed Tahitian dress to fit their westernized concepts of modesty by introducing a patchwork quilted

Figure 4.2. Mormon Mission house at PCC. Photograph by F. Salamone.

fabric, used also for bed covers, burial shrouds and to cloak the bride and groom. Each woman has her own special style in producing these *tifaifai* (Kennett, 1994).

Missionary influence has also been strong in New Zealand. Maori women still wear traditional style headbands, sometimes with feathers and *tiki,* their sacred pendants. Since the Maori had no looms, they use a kind of finger weaving termed *taaniko*. Maori use red, black and white for traditional garb. Missionaries ended most tattooing. Therefore, for ceremonial events, men now use paint to simulate the former tatoos. Men have adapted the bandolier, woven in patterns by *taaniko*. The bandolier was inspired by nineteenth century soldiers. Women now wear a bodice, introduced by missionaries ever-vigilant for the preservation of female modesty (Kennett, 1994). The *piupiu*, or grass skirt, is a traditional item of clothing that is still worn and continues to be made from flax fastened to a waistband. These strands are dyed in *whiinau* bark and are treated in a manner to produce startling patterns. These skirts are made to produce rustling noises which the Maori use as an intrinsic part of their dancing (Kennett, 1994).

Mageo (1996) indicates that Samoan girls changed their hairstyles to placate Christian, mainly Mormon, missionaries. Traditionally, girls shaved their heads and left a lock hanging to indicate restrained sexuality. In contrast, long hair hanging loosely and dyed red indicated sexuality. Interestingly, both styles indicated that a girl was a virgin and ready for marriage; the second style, however, indicated a greater readiness for sexual activity. Today girls wear their hair long to show their virginity and their assertion of free choice in marriage.

Shennan's (1997) description of the Pacific Arts Dance Festival in Samoa indicates the impact of more authentic Polynesian dress and dance from her anthropological perspective. She notes full-length costumes of woven *pandanus*. These costumes had bright gold overskirts. The skirts were dyed and had a spicy aroma. Coconut oil was spread on the bodies.

Clark (1994) describes the manner in which clothing and use of the body are used by Tahitians to distinguish themselves from the French. The key items of clothing used to stress Maohi (Tahitian) identity are the *hei* (garland) and *pareu* (a one-by-two yard of decorated cloth). In addition to clothing, Tahitian bodies 'carry situations,' according to Clark. The body is the center of all social issues and various hygienic and medical practices distinguish the Maori body from the French.

Finally, Polynesia is a geographic area in which tapa cloth predominates. Hauser-Schaublin (1996) indicates that weaving was not generally known in Polynesia. This bark cloth was draped around people and its removal was ritually regulated. It led to a whole set of aesthetics unique to Polynesians. Specifically, Hauser-Schaublin (1996) notes that cloth can be used to tie kinship groups together, represent life and death and tie generations together. Cloth can also be used to reveal and conceal identities as well as values. It is generally worn in a manner that reveals rather than conceals. It accentuates graceful movement, generally related to conceptions of sexuality, at least in Western perspectives.

Polynesians hold a special place in Mormon teaching. Mormons believe that they are part of the lost tribes of Israel (Winchester, 1994). Therefore, Mormons are committed to saving them. They have, for example, converted 30,000 Western Samoans over the last twenty years (Winchester, 1994).

Figure 4.3. Marquessan men performing at PCC's Marquessan Village.
Photograph by F. Salamone

Therefore, deviations in approved dress are especially troubling in the islands. Scholars at BYU-Hawai'i relate stories of Mormon officials who have visited the islands and been disturbed by meeting with devout Mormons who were not dressed in a manner they deemed appropriate. Although males are allowed to be more revealing in their dress at the Center than females, a reflection of the patriarchal nature of Mormon beliefs, there are limits of tolerance and these limits, at least in the stories, are sometimes exceeded in the field. Moreover, Mormons are quite insistent on female virtue being associated with modesty. Modesty and chastity are conflated in traditional Mormon notions of female virtue.

In *Presentation of Self in Everyday Life* (1959), Erving Goffman discussed the concepts of 'frontstage' and 'backstage' in his dramaturgical view of social life. The backstage area is the location where as T. S. Eliot notes, one prepares a face to meet the faces that one encounters in daily life and where people can be 'off-duty' and reveal their true selves. The frontstage is the area in which the play of life occurs. Certainly, observation of the backstage area at the Center reveals an interesting attitude on the part of many youth. They know what prevailing mores are in the wider society. They also know the relationship in the popular mind between Polynesians and eroticism and the depiction of Polynesians and their dress in the media as free from bourgeois inhibitions. They are also well aware of the demands of the Mormon Church regarding propriety; the compromises made by the Center in the interests of attracting tourists and not straying over-much from Mormon sensibilities regarding modesty. In response to a statement by a Polynesian stripper who had once worked at PCC as a student, Stanton stated that he was bewildered by those who criticize the dress at the Center since it is so much more modest than that found in the shows depicting Polynesian dancing on Waikiki. Students (performers) react to these anomalies in a number of ways.

In the backstage area, for example, they can be seen loosening their costumes after the performance, or, in some cases, before it. They mock the lyrics of the songs or pageants in which they have appeared and tell interested tourists the 'real' stories of what they have depicted. If they come from the islands in whose pageants they perform, they will often ad-lib their parts, straying from the written scripts and adding inside information to their cultural presentations. They also vary their dance routines to make them more authentic and, in Western eyes, more suggestive.

These subversions of the text are familiar to those who have studied tourism and the reactions of marginalized peoples and those at power disadvantages. The interesting innovation here is the use of the body to fight back, however quietly, in asserting one's independence and uniqueness. The grace and fluidity of the Polynesian body is an integral part of the Polynesian conception of reality, the individual, the community and world view. This struggle to maintain control of the definition of one's own identity is crucial.

Maccannell (1984, pp. 388–9) has noted the dangers inherent in losing control to others. There is a strong danger that a group can be locked into a touristic image of itself and become an object. Lose of control of self-definition can lead to problems in interacting with other groups. Keeping control of the image it projects is essential to a group's integrity and ability to continue as a viable unit of society.

Bodily Displays at the Polynesian Cultural Center

Tongans joked about having to come to BYU-Hawai'i in order to learn the Tongan game they performed at PCC. They said that in Tonga only members of the royal family play the game. They indicated that this was but one of the subtleties not shared normally with tourists. Another subtlety is the fact that the layout of the islands at the Center is not in the exact configuration that it is in nature.

Robinson (1991) questions the authenticity of the Polynesian Cultural Center. The broader issue is, of course, authenticity for whom? (Salamone, 1997, p. 319). There are elements of authenticity in any cultural performance, although its historical accuracy may be questionable. People have a way of asserting themselves even in performances scripted by others as I argue (1997) with regard to the performance at the San Angel Inn in Disney World. So, too, the performances at the Polynesian Cultural Center provide numerous opportunities to observe 'authentic' attitudes toward the body on the part of the performers and the administrators of the Polynesian Cultural Center.

Knowlton (1992, p. 20) notes that Mary Douglas argues that societies often seek to hide their basic organizing categories, thereby removing them from conscious consideration. This process makes them seem part of the natural order of things, something handed down by a power outside society itself. Douglas contends that Western concepts of the nature of gender is just such an example. We hide the arbitrary nature of the categories through ascribing their creation to God.

Knowlton builds on this concept and uses Gilmore's (1990) notion of the construction of male identity in order to clarify Mormon concepts of gender. He notes that since Mormons do not live in isolation their gender concepts are a mixture of Mormon and broader American constructs. Basically, the belief that male and female gender roles are divinely ordained is the foundation of these beliefs. Mormonism is a male dominated religion in which maleness and religion are seen as inseparable. There is a series of rites of passage to ease young men into preconceived adult male roles. Each boy is trained to desire to go on a mission and to marry soon after so that he may become a patriarch.

Knowlton (1992, p. 26) sums up his position on the conflict between Mormon male sexual values and those of American society by noting the manner in which sexual prowess is a marker for achieving masculinity. However, American notions of masculinity are at odds with traditional Mormon ones. Thus, there is an inevitable conflict between belonging to American society and being in conformity with Church standards. Knowlton argues that this conflict has a psychological cost for Mormons.

In return for their allegiance to Mormon doctrine, men will demand from the Church beliefs and practices to support a male-centered view of religion that will aid them to live up to this ideal. The Church is expected to stress male experiences and attitudes. Thus, masculinity and religion become ever more intertwined. Not surprisingly, the role of women is limited to the extent that the position of men is exalted. Knowlton notes that the expected conflicts between Mormon men and women has materialized and relates numerous examples from his own Mormon experience. One way in which these attitudes and conflicts emerge is in the Mormon sponsored performances at the Polynesian Cultural Center, in which male aggressiveness is stressed and female docility praised. The costumes used at the PCC support the basic Mormon patriarchal structure.

Ferre (1988, p. 42–3) makes it clear that from the beginning, the PCC perceived a need to make the dances more dramatic, in spite of the Center's proclaimed desire to preserve and present 'authentic' Polynesian dances and other cultural exhibits. Michel M. Grilikhes was the Night Show's first director and a major Hollywood choreographer at the time. He stated that after praising the Maori dancers, he told them, 'You've got a problem and the problem is that you're still performing it the way you've always performed it and you've got to have pacing and . . . a story '(quoted in Ferre, 1988, p. 42). Grilikhes helped the Maori to fix their 'problem.' However, from the beginning there was opposition to this Hollywood influence. Future Night Shows have borne Grilikhes's show business stamp ever since.

The support of the Mormon Church and its control over the students who participate in the show are crucial to the Center's success. In turn, the Church expects the show to turn a profit. Mormon academics have been unrelenting in their demand that showmanship be matched with authenticity (Stanton, 1989). These pressures have influenced what happens in the Center, including the manner in which the body is displayed.

In his brief history of the Polynesian Cultural Center, Robert O'Brien (1983) contrasts the beaches filled with bikini-clad beauties with the family and religious values of the Center, the Temple and BYU-Hawai'i. The Center's values are contrasted with normal show business values. In light of Knowlton's comments on Mormon masculinity and its ties to Mormon religiosity, it is interesting to note the difference in dress between male and female 'Polynesians,' although some are not Polynesians except in a show business sense. Men tend to be more scantily clad than women in every setting in which the two appear.

Women tend to be more modestly covered than men. Still, even though scripted in their performance, hula dancers do tend to add a bit more to the hulas they perform. There are sly twinkles in their eyes as they attempt to put a bit more authenticity into their work, given the limits of a family show at a religiously-sponsored center. Tahitian women, for example, stray from the monotonous choreographed footwork and return to the greater freedom of their traditional hula. When these deviations from the script are brought to their attention in interviews, performers tend to shrug and smile.

The Night Show illustrates many of the major points regarding attitudes toward bodily display current among American Mormons and Polynesians. The videotape *Mana: Spirit of Our People* is a convenient presentation of a typical Night Show. It features six of the island cultures: Hawai'i, Fiji, Samoa, Tonga, the Maori and Tahiti. In each segment, men's bodies are more on display than women's. Women are typically covered up in longer clothes with a more modern Hawaiian flavor. As colorful as these clothes are, they do not strike one as traditionally Polynesian, for they have the look of tailored clothing, manufactured for the tourist trade. The pandanas leaves of Samoa seem but a remote memory.

Nevertheless, the manner in which the women drape these dresses over their bodies and the gracefulness in which they move assert their heritage. Moreover, when non-Polynesians in the show wear these dresses they move in a fashion that is stiffer, more in keeping with Euro-American culture, a style Charles Keil (personal communication) terms vertical rather than horizontal. In sum, the Polynesian women flow.

The men are freer to display their bodies and their 'masculinity.' Such openness would be in conformity with Knowlton's comments on Mormon masculinity. It is hard, however, to imagine these Polynesian Mormon men being accused of the frigidity that Knowlton asserts American Mormon women accuse Mormon men of displaying. Their sexuality is apparent and their humor regarding it is quite open. When Sielu, a Samoan chief, displays his prowess in a fire dance, he quite overtly thrusts his fire stick between his legs, representing a burning phallus. As Knowlton mentions, Mormons are surrounded by phallic symbols in their religious imagery, including the architecture of their temples. However, American Mormons are a bit more subtle and shy about these images.

Sielu is also being a bit more open than the other Samoan fire dancers who appear to endanger their genitals through sitting on fire with their grass skirts. The fire dance in this form is, interestingly, only performed by men at the Polynesian Cultural Center. Maori women perform their fire dance with burning balls and in a quieter tempo. The symbolism, however, is rather open and the gracefulness of the women quite sensual.

Attempts to mask or tame the sensuality of Polynesian women do not succeed. Against the writings of Maugham, Melville, London and others, they even appear comic and a sense of *deja vu* overwhelms the commentator. Missionaries have been so satirized by great and not-so-great authors for their imposition of Mother Hubbards and similar dresses that little effort seems required to analyze their failure. The gracefulness in movement that is so integral a characteristic of Polynesian identity defeats even the strictest dress code. These rhythms, moreover, as reinforced by the island dances aid in an internalization of island values while encouraging their external manifestation in appropriate dance movements. A communication system is thereby established that is self-reinforcing.

There is also an unselfconscious treatment of the body that is an integral part of the Polynesian sense of self. Although the women's costumes are not traditionally authentic, women mold themselves to them and thereby make them their own. The costumes are, as already stated, in the colorful tradition of the islands and they are flowing and graceful as used by the island women. Their carriage and grace further incorporate the dress into their own cultural tradition. They have assimilated the articles in conformity with their own use of them.

Men's clothing, even the more 'modern' notions of Polynesian dress, are worn skin-tight without any censure by the Saints. Constant reminders of the Center's ties with the Latter Day Saints mark the videotape, reflecting the situation at the Center. In contrast, there is great care taken not to reveal, on stage, any part of a female breast. This differential concern with the display of secondary sexual characteristics is, according to Knowlton, a marked feature of Mormon ideology and an 'innate' and divinely ordained difference in the sexes.

The aggressiveness that men are allowed to display in their dances, contrasted with the apparent subservience of women and their docility is also in conformity with Mormon beliefs although not traditionally part of all Polynesian cultures. In Tonga, female aggression is allowed expression in limited contexts. However, women use a number of occasions to display covert aggression, even speeches on Christian charity if need be (Olson, 1994, p. 237–8). Display of aggression is a sign of freedom and Tongan women jealously guard their freedom.

Therefore, it is not surprising that both men and women subvert the characteristics they are supposed to display at the PCC. The 'fierce' Fijian chief, a former schoolteacher, often breaks out into a broad smile when encouraging his people. Sielu, whose fire dance is about equal parts modern and traditional, presents a softer image in his much-prized dialogues, affecting an effeminate voice that draws generous laughs and applause and intentionally mocks an overdone macho ideal. In personal conversation, he is a thoughtful and considerate person with enormous patience and charm.

Women are not allowed to be so open in their sensuality as the men. Even the Tahitian hula, the most demonstrative of all the hulas in the Center, is performed with long grass skirts by the women, not in the traditional short skirts and topless. The men are allowed to wear shorter skirts and are mainly topless. The Center advertises the Tahitian hula as the one most tourists confuse with all hulas; namely, the one in which they expect swaying hips. This allowing of openly sensual hip movement is a concession to the tourists and is contained by a number of factors: the length of the skirt, the relatively briefness of the performance, an appeal to the cultural nature of the authentic hula and a kind of good-natured fun. The performance, however, is regularly subverted by the sensuousness of the performers. There is once again a delight in the body that is rare among most Americans. It strikes one as an open, healthy attitude, one that overcomes strict dress codes and moral codes that seek to inhibit bodily expression through binding it in suffocating rules and restrictions.

Both men and women seek to subvert the restrictive rules that on one level they have accepted but on another attack their self-identity. Open rebellion is out of the question, for it would jeopardize their income and education as well as any future advancement with which the Mormon Church would offer them. It is also arbitrary to question the legitimate adherence that many of these young adults and their elders feel to the Mormon Church. Nonetheless, it is obvious that these youngsters use their bodies to put forth a different definition of self than that imposed on them through the Mormon faith. Their body language speaks volumes and aids in their subversion of a dictated reality.

Conclusion

An exploration that focuses on the body goes far in understanding the distinctive place that a particular people have in the world. Moore (1994, p. 17), for example, states 'Bodies. It all has to do with bodies.' She argues for a movement beyond the obvious male–female differences in body toward an embodied concord and correspondence. Examination of the manner in which bodies are displayed in the Polynesian Cultural Center has moved us toward her position. The differences in the conception of the body's meaning between Mormons and Polynesians, moreover, has alerted us to the manner in which 'physicality ' is used in the politics of local hermeneutics (Broche-Due, 1993). Attention to the use of the body at the Polynesian Cultural Center, further-more, reinforces the phenomenological fact that real people are involved in manipulating their bodies to make statements about their own experiences within cultural contexts.

In Lock's (1993) perceptive argument they are using a resocialized body to express their independence. This body has created itself thorough the use of subjective emotions in 'dialogue with or subjugated by social practice and knowledge' (Worthman, 1993, p. 161). Lock exhorts subjugated people to 'resist all pressures from the Other to produce tidy answers and 'Just So stories' (1993, p. 148). In other words, she calls for a raising of consciousness about what has happened to them and for them to seek a means to define their own identities through a 'dialogue' with their own bodily and cultural experiences.

Lock reminds us that, going back to Durkheim, there is a social science tradition that has approached the problem of the body in a manner seeking to understand the relationship between the 'universal physical body and the 'higher' morally-imbued 'socialized' body ' (Lock 1993, p. 135; Durkheim 1961). This tradition has yielded useful insights through Mauss (1935) and Van Gennep (1960), both of whom insisted on the relationship between physical, psychosocial and social domains. Additionally, Van Gennep's work on ritual demonstrated that body techniques relate closely to the way in which culture maps time and space.

Many who have followed in that tradition have shown close relationships between the manner in which cultures structure social thought and symbols and the body. These systems of thought are seen as 'natural' by those who hold them, as well as 'universal' in application. Freud and Levi-Strauss, of course, have made similar arguments that reflect the folk wisdom of many societies among whom anthropologists have worked.

Although a structuralist in her own right, Mary Douglas has argued persuasively that 'every 'natural' expression is culturally determined' (Lock 1993, p. 136). Perhaps, that flat assertion requires modification in light of other studies that look at color discrimination and other physically tied perceptions. However, in the major areas in which she works, she is more right than wrong. Others have added to her work, and we are now more concerned with the manner in which the body functions as a sender and receiver of information. Again, this study of the Polynesian Cultural Center has sought to address this problem through attention to the performances in the Night Show and in other areas at the Center.

Jackson's (1989, p. 131) work has called our attention to the role of imitation (mimesis) in social life and in understanding the social importance of the body. He sees the creative freedom found in mimetic play as being bounded by the cultural environment, or habitus. The way in which the body is used, he argues, generates ideas and inculcate moral predispositions. These practices bring about a personal understanding of social values.

Finally, Lock notes those studies concerned with peripheral peoples and the manner in which the body becomes a means for dissent. Work by Camaroff, Obeyesekere and others has alerted us to the role that the body plays in the performance of social life and how that performance can be a means for dissent. Certainly, the actual performances at the Polynesian Cultural Center express a dialectical definition of Polynesian identity in contrast to that which is programmed.

References

Arthur, L. B. (1998). Fossilized fashion in Hawai'i. *Paideusis; Journal of Inter-disciplinary Cultural Studies (1)*, A15–28.

Arthur, L. B. (1997). Cultural authentication refined: The case of the Hawaiian holoku. *Clothing and Textiles Research Journal, 15 (3)*, 129–39.

Arthur, L. B. (1998). Fossilized fashion in Hawai'i. *Paideusis; Journal of Inter-disciplinary Cultural Studies. (1).* A15–A28.

Broche-Due, V. (1993). Making meaning out of matter: Perceptions of sex, gender and bodies among the Turkana. In V. Broch-Due, I. Rudie and T. Bleie (eds.), *Carved flesh/cast selves: Gendered symbols and social practices* (pp. 53–82). Oxford: Berg.

Clark, S. (1994) Ethnicity embodied: evidence from Tahiti. *Ethnology 33 (3)*, 211–27.

Cook, O. (n.d.) Publicity releases for the hukilau. Laie, HI: Polynesian Cultural Center.

Douglas, M. (1966). *Purity and danger.* London: Routledge.

Douglas, M. (1973). *Natural symbols.* New York: Random House.

Durkheim, E. (1961). *The elementary forms of the religious life.* J. W. Swain. New York: Collier.

Fact Sheet (1997). Polynesian Culture Center. Http://www.polynesia.com/pcc/Info/Fact.html.

Feast Follows Fishing At Real Native hukilau. (1969, May 30–June 1. 1969). *Waikiki Beach Press.*

Ferre, C. (1988). *A history of the Polynesian Cultural Center's 'Night Show': 1963–1983.* A Dissertation presented to the Department of Theatre and Film. Brigham Young University, August 1988.

Geertz, C. (1980). Blurred genres: The refiguration of social thought. *American Scholar, 29*, 165–79.

Gilmore, D. (1990). *Manhood in the making: Cultural concepts of masculinity.* New Haven: Yale U. Press.

Goffman, E. (1959). *The presentation of self in everyday life.* Garden City: Doubleday.

Hauser-Schaublin, B. (1996). The thrill of the line, the string and the frond, or why the Abelam are a non-cloth culture. *Oceania, 67* (2): 81–106.

Jackson, M. (1989). *Paths toward a clearing: Radical empiricism and ethnographic Inquiry.* Bloomington: University of Indiana Press.

Kawahigashi, K. (1968). The Hukilau Festival of January 31, 1948. Unpublished paper. BYU-Hawai'i.

Kennett, F. (1994). *Ethnic Dress.* New York: Facts on File.

Knowlton, D. (1992). On Mormon masculinity. *Sunstone, 13*, 19–31.

Lock, M. (1993). Cultivating the body: Anthropology and epistemologies of bodily practice and knowledge. *Annual Review of Anthropology, 22*, 133–55.

Maccannell, D. (1984). Reconstructed ethnicity: Tourism and cultural identity in third world communities. *Annals of Tourism Research, 11*, 375–91.

Manning, F. (1986). Forward. In R. Swiderski (ed.) *Voices* (pp. vii–viii). Bowling Green, OH: Popular Culture Press.

Mauss, M. (1935). The techniques of the body. Translated 1973 in *Economic Sociology, 2*, 70–88.

Moore, H. L. (1993). The differences within and the differences between. In T. del Valle (ed.) *Gendered Anthropology.* (pp. 193–219). London: Routledge.

Mageo, J. M. (1996). Hairdos and don'ts: Hair symbolism and sexual history in Samoa. *Frontiers 17 (2)*: 138–57.

O'Brien, R. (1983). *Hands across the water*. Laie, HI: Polynesian Cultural Center.

Olson, E. (1994) Female voices of aggression in Tonga. *Sex Roles: A Journal of Research, 30*, 237–48.

Polynesian Cultural Center. (1992). *Mana: Spirit of Our People*. Videotape, Laie, HI.

Robinson, A. M. (1991). The Polynesian Cultural Center: A study of authenticity. *The Chico Anthropology Society Papers, 13*, 21–53.

Salamone, F. A. (1997). Authenticity in tourism: The San Angel Inns. *Annals of Tourism Research, 24*, 305–21.

Shennan, J. (1997). Pacific overtures. (1996 Pacific Arts Festival). *Dance, 7 (1)*, 52–54.

Siufanua, P. (1990). Oh We're Going to a hukilau. Unpublished paper, BYU Hawai'i.

Stanton, M. (1977). The Polynesian Cultural Center: Presenting Polynesia to the world or the world to Polynesia. In B. R. Finney and K. A. Watson (eds.). *A New Kind of Sugar* (pp. 229–33). Honolulu: The East-West Center.

Stanton, M. (1989). The Polynesian Cultural Center: A multi-ethnic model of seven Pacific cultures. In V. Smith (ed.) *Hosts and Guests: The Anthropology of Tourism* (pp. 247–264). Philadelphia: University of Pennsylvania Press.

Swiderski, R. (1986). *Voices*. Bowling Green, OH: Popular Culture Press.

VanGennep, A. (1960). *The rites of passage*. Trans. M. B. Vizedom and G. L. Caffee. Chicago: University of Chicago Press.

Winchester, S. (1994). Saving the Samoans. (Mormon evangelism in Western Samoa). *Mother Jones, 19 (1)*, 13–14.

Worthman, C. (1993) Cupid and psyche: Investigative syncretism in biological and psychosocial anthropology. In G. Schwartz, White, G. F. and Lutz, K. (eds). *The social life of psyche: Debates and direction in psychological anthropology* (pp. 150–78). Cambridge: Cambridge University Press.

5

The Obedient and Disobedient Daughters of the Church: Strangite Mormon Dress as a Mode of Control

Gayle Veronica Fischer

In June 1851, James Jesse Strang and several of his Latter Day Saint (Strangite Mormon) followers were charged with counterfeiting, trespassing on federal lands and obstructing the US mail. District Attorney George Bates, determined to discredit the Mormon witnesses, battered the Strangites with questions about their allegiance to 'King' Strang and their disregard for laws that did not come directly from him. The deposition of Sarah McCulloch dramatically illustrates the faith Strang's followers had in him. Before reproducing the records, Bates inaccurately and maliciously described the Mormons in attendance as a 'motley crowd with the ladies in full bloomer costume, Strang in his pontifical robes' (Bates, 1903, p. 233). Although we must be skeptical of the accuracy of the transcription from which the following is drawn, McCulloch's assertions nevertheless demonstrate Strang's charisma:

Question – 'Mrs McCulloch, you are an educated, accomplished lady born in Baltimore and reared in the very best society. Can it be that you are a Mormon?'
Answer – 'Yes, sir, I have that honor, sir.'
Q. – 'Can it be possible, madam, that so accomplished a lady as you are can believe that that fellow Strang is a prophet, seer and revelator?'
A . – 'Yes, Mr District Attorney, I know it.'
Q. – 'Can it be possible, Mrs McCulloch, that you are so blind as to really believe that that fellow who sits there beneath you – that Strang, is the Prophet of the Lord, the successor of him who bore his cross among the jeers and sneers of Mount Calvary?'

A. – 'Yes, you impudent district attorney and were you not a darned old fool you would know it too!' (Bates, 1903, p. 233–4).

The jury acquitted Strang and his disciples. Ironically, Sarah McCulloch would, a few short years later, rail against his command that all women wear the 'Mormon' dress, becoming one of his most outspoken detractors. Although Bates (1903) recalled the Strangite women as wearing 'bloomer costumes,' few, if any, would have been wearing bloomers at this early date.

Around 1850 a new style was introduced to women in the United States: the 'bloomer costume,' so named in 1851, consisted of trousers worn beneath a shortened full-skirted gown. The bloomer outfit never appealed to the majority of American women and of the few who did wear it most abandoned it after a brief trial. Surprisingly, the dress found a following in various communal and alternative religious organizations. Members of new religions often considered themselves to be a new version of the chosen people; although they frequently sanctioned a change in dress for symbolic reasons, few religions chose bloomers as their 'uniforms' (Lauer and Lauer, 1983). In this chapter, I look at how James Jesse Strang, leader of the Strangite Mormons, used a bloomer-type garment as a mechanism to control his followers, especially the women. I begin with a brief discussion of patriarchy and how the Strangite religious community fits into my understanding of patriarchy. I then provide the reader with an overview of Mormonism and show where Strangite Mormons fit into this larger movement. This section is followed by a biography of James Jesse Strang, the origins of Strangite Mormonism and a comparison of some of the similarities between Strangite and Utah Mormonism. The circumstances under which bloomer-style garments made their way into Strang's vision for his followers and their reactions to the dress and Strang's desires make up the majority of this chapter. Undergirding this historical narrative is an analysis of how women's bodies are controlled through their dress and how this social control can be used by those in positions of power to secure their dominant place. In this case, James Jesse Strang dictated to women what they could wear in an effort to prove that as 'King of Beaver Island,' Michigan, he could control the most intimate aspects of his followers lives.

Strang and the Strangite Mormons did not depart from the basic notions of patriarchy in nineteenth-century US society. The Strangite community on Beaver Island originated with a man, as a male construct with women defined by their relationships to men. Strang's visions were grounded in the pervasive ideology of patriarchal power. Patriarchy can be narrowly defined as the power of the father over his wife, children and other dependents. In some ways this definition can be aptly applied to the Strangite community which was founded and controlled by a charismatic man who married five women and had many children. The patriarchal order on Beaver Island consisted of a system in which Strang and a chosen few used direct and indirect pressure, laws and religious ritual to determine what women would wear and they were unprepared when some women resisted.

Mormonism

In the 1820s, Joseph Smith found golden tablets with 'The Book of Mormon' inscribed on them. His supporters believed that he had been especially chosen by God to restore 'true' Christianity (Foster, 1991). A teaching central to the Mormon doctrine (as revealed to Smith), was that the Latter Day Saints were living in the final dispensation of the Gospel. This was a time of preparation for the resurrection of the ancient Saints and the return of Jesus Christ to begin his millennial reign in God's kingdom on earth. The headquarters for the Church of Jesus Christ of Latter Day Saints was established eventually in Nauvoo, Illinois, which initially welcomed Smith and his followers and granted them a good deal of autonomy. Many of the distinctive features of Mormon theology date from the Nauvoo period: the plurality of Gods, baptism for the dead, marriage for eternity and plural marriage. Smith also created the controversial Council of Fifty, permitted the establishment of a Masonic Temple (a secret organization) and borrowed from Masonic rituals to establish the secret rituals of the Mormon temple (Moore, 1986).

One of the Nauvoo Mormons secrets was a sacred white garment referred to as 'the garment of the Holy Priesthood.' The garment was worn by participants in a religious ceremony that had theological instruction as its main focus. At this secret ceremony 'endowments' were given as a step toward being accepted into the 'Celestial Kingdom.'[1] Although originally designed as an undergarment for the endowment ceremonies, the garment was worn beneath regular clothing (and next to the skin) everyday afterward (McDannell, 1995). The sacred garment probably resembled today's contemporary long underwear or a union suit. Unlike most religious apparel, which made church affiliation visible, it was secret and invisible to the casual observer, allowing the wearer alone 'to keep the faith.'

The innovations and the secrecy Smith introduced to Mormonism eventually worked against the religion in Illinois, turning public opinion against the Mormons as well as creating internal dissension. The Mormon secrets turned to rumors, and popular gossip in Illinois hinted at Mormon conspiracies to disrupt the economic and political life of the state (Moore, 1986). After Joseph Smith was killed, a number of groups broke away from the main body of Mormons. One group became the Reorganized Church of Latter Day Saints and stayed faithful to the Book of Mormon but rejected Smith's ideas about gathering, secret temple rituals and the doctrine of plural marriage. Although this group survived, it did not prosper to the same degree as the Mormons who journeyed to Utah under the leadership of Brigham Young. Another splinter group – the Strangite Mormons – will be discussed below.

James Jesse Strang and Strangite Theology

By the time he was thirty, James Jesse Strang had worked as a farmer, taught school, given temperance lectures, practiced law, dabbled in politics, edited a newspaper and served as a postmaster. He married Mary Abigail Perce in 1836 and together they had four children. Seven years later, Strang and his family followed the lead of many others in the country and moved west to Burlington, Wisconsin. Shortly thereafter, Mormon missionaries persuaded him to visit Nauvoo, Illinois, Joseph Smith's Mormon community. In February 1844, Strang received religious instruction, was baptized, became a Mormon church elder and was given a ministry in Wisconsin. Strang spread the word of Smith's Church – but he also had some ideas of his own that he wished to plant.[2]

Joseph Smith was assassinated in June 1844 and Strang – a Mormon convert for only about six months – insisted on his right to succeed Smith. Strang claimed to have had a divine vision at the very hour of Smith's murder, to have received a letter from Smith written nine days before his death and to have unearthed three ancient brass plates. All of these were considered signs that purportedly recognized him as the new leader of God's chosen people. The struggle for the succession ended in the triumph of Brigham Young and the excommunication of Strang. Not one to easily accept defeat, Strang returned to Wisconsin and continued to assert his position as he gathered a small body of believers around him – the Strangite Mormons.

On August 25, 1846, Strang had a vision that described Big Beaver Island in northern Lake Michigan as the future home of the Strangite Saints, or Strangite Mormons. The island, twenty-five miles from the mainland, offered Strangite Mormons isolation from powerful outside forces and protection from their detractors and enemies as well as a place to live and prosper and practice their faith freely. The settlement on Beaver Island, including the village of St. James, grew; in the summer of 1849 more than 250 Strangite Saints had located there and by 1850 that number had more than tripled.[3] 'King Strang' was 'prophet, seer, revelator, translator and first president of the

seem a logical choice given the physical environment they traversed. Perhaps one of the best descriptions of Brighamite 'deseret dress' comes from the travel letters of Mrs Benjamin Ferris:

> I readily recognize her old yellow marten fur cape – her wide cap-border flapping in the wind, under a comical-looking hood – and her dress, some of her own handiwork in spinning and weaving, just wide enough and none to spare, around her gaunt frame. This notable dress is Bloomer enough to display a servicable pair of brogans [heavy work shoe] (Ferris, 1856, p. 156).

Several descriptions of the Strangite dress are extant. An observer described Strangite 'ladies in full bloomer costume' (Bates, 1903, p. 233). Decades later, a chronicler also employed the descriptive shorthand, Strangite 'women were required to wear bloomers' (Campbell, 1906, p. 135). *Harper's New Monthly Magazine* noted 'All the [Strangite] women were compelled to wear the short skirts and ample pantalets of the Bloomer costume' (March 1882, p. 557). Utley stated that ' Strang ordered all the women of his kingdom to wear 'bloomers,' that is oriental trousers, just then advocated by a Mrs Bloomer of New York' (1906, p. 306–7). Shortly after the term was coined in 1851, 'bloomer' became the catch-all phrase for describing any female outfit that consisted of a shortened skirt with exposed trousers beneath. Any nineteenth-century reader would have known immediately what the term 'bloomer costume' meant and this may explain the dearth of more elaborate descriptions of Strangite 'Mormon' dress or Brighamite 'deseret dress' – saying 'bloomers' said it all (see Figure 5.1).

We should not be surprised to learn that Strangite Saints and Brighamite Saints experimented with outer clothing in their relatively new religions. The popular nineteenth-century American notion that God had created the human form in his divine image led some reformers and religious leaders to argue, paradoxically, that the body should be clothed to keep it in its 'natural' or 'consecrated' state. While they sought to maintain the body God wanted them to have, many believers also drew on literature that blamed the Fall on Eve and linked sin, the body, woman and clothing to campaign for changes in female dress. Finery in general had long been considered a vice in many Christian religions and this was true among the Utah and Beaver Island Mormons as well. Strang (1856) denounced extravagant, impractical female fashion, just as many critics before him had. The desire for beautiful clothing was an urge that women had to control and if they could not exercise restraint on their own then Strang would 'help' them to combat their appetite for the frivolous. No doubt Strang would have agreed with Angelina Merritt's assessment that women's 'devotion to fashions' rendered them 'unworthy of

SCENES IN AN AMERICAN HAREM.

BRIGHAM YOUNG AND HIS FAMILY ON THEIR WAY TO CHURCH.

Figure 5.1. Although the caption states that this Brigham Young and some of his wives, it is highly unlikely that this picture is accurate due to the date. By 1857 most bloomer-wearers had given up the costume, especially those who had been only marginally interested such as the Utah Mormons. In this illustration, the deseret costumes look remarkably like the bloomer costume in Figure 5.2. The illustration is useful as an example of the subtle variations between costumes such as the deseret, the Mormon, and the bloomer which made it impossible to tell the outfits apart. *(Harper's Weekly* 10 October 1857, p. 648).

their immortal natures' (Merritt, 1852, p. 110–1). By changing the outer garments of women, Strang gave the world visible proof that his followers could control their earthy and bodily urges and passions.

A similar objective of controlling worldly longing for fashionable dresses led Brigham Young and Eliza R. Snow, sometime in the 1850s, to encourage Utah Mormon women to find a 'stabilised dress' (Gates, 1930). The design they came up with, the deseret dress, consisted of 'bloomers and full skirts, without hoops, trimming or trains.' Apparently the outfit was worn by Brighamite women primarily on their travels to Utah and in the early settlement period. The unattractive, 'hideous' dress did not appeal to many of the women and within a few years they returned to 'beautiful colours and pretty clothes' (Spencer and Harmer, 1940, p. 85–6). The Utah Mormons never invested as much time or thought in the deseret garment as the Strangite Mormons spent on their 'Mormon' dresses (Walkup, 1947).

It is worth looking at the Oneida Community, which developed amidst the religious enthusiasm sweeping over western New York in the first half of the nineteenth century and their dress experiments to better understand how dress can be used in a religious context to control women. Oneida shared several features with the Strangites, the most obvious being the presence of a strong, dynamic leader – John Humphrey Noyes. The charismatic Noyes (like Strang) ruled with a firm hand and based his authority on divine inspiration. Prohibitions on alcohol, narcotics and small shoes, boots and waists were based on a rudimentary understanding of health issues. Today, Oneida is best known for 'complex marriage,' 'male continence,' 'mutual criticism,' 'stirpiculture' – and the dress of Community women.[6] The alternative costume Oneida women wore has been described as similar to 'the dress of children – frock and pantalettes' (*First Annual Report,* 1849). With the encouragement of Noyes, Community women followed the example of prominent female members until frocks and loose pantalettes became the typical attire in the Community. Oneida women willingly wore the new outfit rather than risk Noyes's displeasure.

No official rule ever made the Oneida short dress compulsory – in contrast, Strang would eventually *order* his female followers to wear Mormon dress. There is no 'hard' evidence that Strang knew of Oneida's short dress, but it is plausible that he learned of the Community and their clothing in his travels east. The closed religious community with its authoritative male leader may have reinforced Strang's philosophy and its female dress may have suggested possibilities that he had not yet considered. The New York-born Strang left the state in 1843, five years before the Oneidans experimented with dress; therefore he could only have learned of the dress after his conversion to Mormonism. It is conceivable that knowledge of Noyes, Oneida and its dress code for women influenced Strang's desire to introduce such an outfit to Strangite Mormon women. Strang, like John Humphrey Noyes, controlled all ecclesiastical, secular and civil affairs within his kingdom; only his endorsement would permit women to wear an outfit that included pants – long believed to be an exclusively male garment.

The bloomer-Strangite-Mormon-deseret-Oneida dress is a mass of contradictions. On the one hand it enabled women to control their passion for finery, yet almost universal opinion in the nineteenth century agreed that the dress was 'ugly' and only a few women would wear a garment they considered unattractive for a sustained period of time. The dress seemed to offer women bodily freedom: escape from constricting corsets, release from confining long skirts and petticoats, emancipation from tight shoes. At the same time that the new dresses offered women physical deliverance, they often bound women to men who dictated their clothing choices, or tied women to clothing that expressed ideologies that they did not necessarily agree with, or opened women up to a new form of dress-based criticism. The short dress and pants in the nineteenth-century United States was all about control; whether women controlled the dress or were controlled by it varied.

Reform Dress, Charles J. Douglas and the Mormon Dress

In a rather odd turn of events, the first time a Strangite Mormon woman wore a dress ordained by Strang, it was a disguise. Strang, his legal wife Mary Perce Strang and their children, traveled east in 1849 to recruit settlers to Beaver Island; Strang also wanted his second and (at that time) secret wife Elvira Eliza Field Strang to accompany him. Strang disguised his young wife as a man, his 'male' secretary. Elvira Field Strang, transformed into Charles J. Douglas with a short haircut and dressed in men's clothing, met Strang in New York and traveled with him spreading the word about Strangite Mormonism. Elvira Field Strang's disguise did not fool everyone: rumors circulated about 'his suspicious curves' and observers saw the Strangs kissing and touching intimately. Mary Perce Strang became aware of her husband's interest in another woman through his curious references to 'Charley Douglas' in his letters (*Northern Islander*, 9 January 1851). At the conclusion of the eastern journey, Strang acknowledged Elvira Field Strang as his wife in polygamy and reversed his earlier stance against the practice. Mary Perce continued to live for a short while on Beaver Island; she then returned to Wisconsin. Her letters suggest that she continued to love Strang even as they lived apart. Ultimately, Strang had three more wives in addition to Mary Perce and Elvira Field.

Although Elvira Strang wore pants as 'Douglas,' this did not directly translate into a new outfit with pants for Strangite women. Strang introduced a 'new Mormon' dress to his female followers, but the accounts of this event (many written years later) often disagree with one another, making it difficult to follow the chronology of dress reform on Beaver Island. The first reference to a distinctive dress worn by female Strangites can be found in the diary of Stephen Post, a Mormon elder. Writing about his trip to the island for a conference in 1850, Post described Elvira Field Strang's 'odd' dress: 'She was dressed in pantalets – long loose trousers gathered closely about the ankles – covered by a skirt that came down to her knees' (Van Noord, 1988, p. 100). Post also learned that this had become the typical style of dress for Beaver Island women. Two facts make this reference particularly fascinating: If Post is correct, then Strangite Saints adopted the reform outfit almost a year before Amelia Bloomer first wore the famed bloomer costume; this reinforces my hypothesis that the most logical place for Strang to have learned of reform dress before deciding on a similar dress for his female followers was at Oneida. In May 1851, the Strangite newspaper the *Northern Islander* carried a brief article about 'short dresses.' It is unclear if the piece was reprinted from another newspaper or if Strang wrote it. The content of the article can be read in two ways. The article mentions 'several ladies' who appeared in Syracuse, New York, in bloomer outfits and notes that Syracuse is a town 'for all kinds of foolish and odd freaks to take root in.' The article continues in this vein, laughing at an outfit similar to one already worn on the island, which seems odd given that the Strangites expressed pride in their reform. If the commentary was reprinted, this implies that the Strangites monitored reactions to the dress in the Gentile world, perhaps as a way of differentiating their own clothing experiences. Or maybe, for them, the secular dress was worth mocking because it was worldly (not divinely ordained) – only the blessing of a king would consecrate what would otherwise be freakish. Despite conflicting or puzzling evidence and stories, it seems reasonable that by the summer of 1852 the 'Mormon dress' was commonplace, but not universal, on Beaver Island (Riegel, 1935; *Northern Islander*). In 1852 Strang, perhaps following the lead of John Humphrey Noyes, did not initially institute strict dress regulations. A few years later, however, he no longer tolerated the informal dress code and formalized rules about dress.

'Apparel and Ornaments'

James Jesse Strang was controversial among his contemporaries – and among historians and biographers who have debated how much control and power Strang had over his followers. The religious leader has been demonized and vilified by those who believe that Strang acted on a desire for personal gain rather than from divine inspiration. The negative assessments tend to focus on the secular and dramatic incidents of life on the island. Strang's defenders, on the other hand, argue for the strength of his faith in God and God's messages and tend to focus their attention on his theology. Lawrence Foster (1981) clearly admires Strang but offers a reasonable assessment of the prophet as a man inspired by faith but who was never able to transcend his earthly ambitions. The extreme judgments of Strang and events on Beaver Island have sometimes led to the manufacturing or distortion of evidence on both sides. In his zeal to defend Strang, Doyle C. Fitzpatrick insists that he was a man ahead of his time even in the area of fashion and that the 'Strangite bloomers' predated Amelia Bloomer's dress by *fifty years* – such an error, however, makes Fitzpatrick's other conclusions suspect (Fitzpatrick, 1970, p. 200–201).[7] George Bates, the lawyer who prosecuted Strang in 1851, may have fabricated most of his 1877 *Detroit Advertiser and Tribune* article, which became the basis for many of the accounts later written about the prophet.[8] Yet this much is beyond debate: Strang did rule his followers with authority and nowhere is this more clearly evidenced than with the Mormon dress.

At a conference in 1855, Strang made remarks 'concerning the apparel of the sisters' that required women to conform to the 'pattern that God [had] given.' He then ordered the women to wear 'full-length calico-pantalets, covered by a matching straight-waisted dress reaching down to the knees' (*Northern Islander*, 9 August 1855). (see Figure 5.2). His directive corresponded with the conclusion of his translation of the brass tablets, which were later published as *The Book of the Law of the Lord*.

Chapter 39, 'Apparel and Ornaments,' of *The Book* began with the injunction, 'Ye shall not clothe yourselves after the manner of the follies of other men; but after the manner that is seemly and convenient, shall ye clothe yourselves' (Strang, 1856, p. 288). The chapter then details objections against female dress and provides some specific clothing instructions. 'King' James's motivations for changing female attire paralleled those of other contemporary dress reformers. Both *The Book* and *The Northern Islander* reiterated arguments that had been in circulation for decades (some for centuries). Strang and Strangite writers railed against the indecency and the vagaries of fashion, which demanded that women sacrifice 'convenience, health and sometimes life' (*Northern Islander* 28 May 1856; 19 May 1856; 14 February 1856). From time to time the island newspaper reprinted the fashion opinions of commentators it agreed with; several of 'Mrs Swisshelm's' comments even found their way in *The Book of the Law of the Lord* – unacknowledged. For example, Swisshelm wrote, 'I notice they [women] are awfully deformed, too, as a general rule, having great lumps on their backs, like dromedaries ' (*Northern Islander* July 1852). *The Book* similarly remarked on skirts 'padded out to the uncouth style of a camel's hump' (Strang, 1856, p. 289). A February 14, 1856, *Northern Islander* article, commenting on hoop skirts, facetiously invited those sisters 'who have itching eyes for Gentile customs' to make haste and adopt the new outrageous fashion or 'they will be too late' and the fashion will have passed. Briefly, chapter 39 lists the problems with 'fashion' as follows: (1) extravagance in ornamentation; (2) constantly changing styles that invite wastefulness; (3) unhealthy and possibly even deadly, fashion encourages depravity among those who follow it; (4) some styles are simply ugly and should not be worn; (5) high fashion promotes class dissension (Strang, 1856). All of these arguments could be found in most dress reform and anti-fashion material, but in 1855 they became a part of official Strangite Latter Day Saint doctrine and heralded a new order for the Beaver Island community.

BLOOMER FASHIONS FOR NOVEMBER.

Figure 5.2. These are exaggeratedly feminine versions of the bloomer costume. Most dress reformers would not have worn the corsets that are clearly creating the nipped in waists on these models. The Mormon costume worn by female Beaver Island Strangites and the deseret costume worn by the Utah Brighamite Mormons would probably have resembled more restrained versions of these outfits (*Peterson's Magazine*, October 1851).

The apparel chapter did not simply outline the objections to Gentile fashions, but also made it clear that the Saints 'shall clothe themselves according to my [Strang's or God's?] Commandment ' (Strang, 1856, p. 290). The 'law' distinguished between clothing worn for public gatherings and formal worship – this dress was a 'matter of divine appointment' – and everyday wear. Although apparel for 'common uses' did not have the distinction of being a 'positively divine appointment,' it continued to be regulated by Commandment (Strang, 1856, p. 290). Within limits Saints could 'exercise [their] own taste in common apparel' – for women this meant customizing Mormon dress (Strang, 1856, p. 290). When proselytizing or traveling among Gentiles, Saints could 'imitate, to some moderate extent, their [Gentile] foolish and ridiculous styles,' in order to avoid being singled out or made the object of ridicule (Strang, 1856, p. 290). Oneida women also wore worldly fashions when they left the confines of their community, which suggests another link between the Strangite and Oneida dress reforms. Because of the hostility often directed at their followers and their beliefs, it is not surprising that Strang and Noyes would want to minimize visual differences outside of their havens; not coincidentally, fashionable dress also made it easier to attract new converts.

In addition to outlining the daily wear of his followers, Strang also introduced uniforms for 'your King and your Princes and your Judges and Rulers . . . and the Priest who administers at the altar' (1856, p. 289). The style of these robes would not be permanent but could change when necessary or divinely ordained. I have been unable to locate information that explains when and how the descriptions of the robes were distributed, nor have I found a description of the robes. The rather strange testimony of Mr Adams at Strang's 1851 trial does, however, suggest some possibilities:

> Q. – 'Well, sir, what position do you hold in this Mormon Church?'
> A. – 'I am one of the apostles, sir. I represent in this church the Apostle Paul, sir.'
> Q. – Well, do you represent that character in costume when you meet with the other officers of Strang's church? . . .'
> A. – 'Yes, sir, when I enact the part of the Apostle Paul in our church I do so in my old theatrical costume of Richard III' (Bates, 1903, p. 234).

To further distinguish officials from one another and from the laity on the island, Strang set up a system of insignia and ornaments. So important was this system, which made the wearer's position or status visible to others, that to transgress the rules was considered a 'high offense' and would result in a 'humiliating punishment' (Strang, 1856, p. 290). As important as the system seemed to be, the directives from Strang often contradicted themselves or were open to interpretation:

> Gold is the proper colour for the Priesthood of an Endless Life and silver for the Priesthood of Life; but other material may be used, having reference to colour and incorruptibility (Strang, 1856, p. 290).

By imposing a strict adherence to uniform regulations, Strang not only made differences in rank and status clear, he also accentuated gender differences: only men could wear the new sacred insignia. Strangite Mormons now literally had to 'go by the book' in matters of dress.

Why did Strang wait to formalize a dress code? It is possible that he hoped to replicate Noyes's success at Oneida, where most of the women wore short dresses without being ordered to do so. That Strang had to put a law in place suggests that his influence was not as strong or widespread as he wanted and that he found it necessary to institutionalize his authority. An underlying motive for reforming Beaver Island Mormon dress may then have been greater social control. Strangite theology came from the mind and life experiences of a mortal man who always retained an awareness of his own ambitions and desire to rule without opposition and Strang used uniformity in dress to gain greater control over his followers, especially the women. A uniform was never adopted for universal wear on Beaver Island, with the exception of formal gatherings and then only those who had specific duties wore prescribed robes.

Uniformity or similarity in dress did, however, become standard on the island. The difference between uniforms and uniformity is significant as well as paradoxical. Uniform wearers are usually encouraged to give up their individuality and act primarily as 'occupants of their uniformed status' (Joseph, 1986, p. 66–75); thus it would seem that if Strang wanted to control every aspect of his followers' lives he would have commanded uniforms rather than uniformity. Yet Strang did not use uniforms to strengthen his authority because to do so would have pushed his followers too far – as the resistance to Mormon dress showed Strang. Standardized apparel enabled Strang to limit and regulate the clothing choices available to women and reinforced his dominance (apparently men did not have to follow the same strict rules women did) without having to go to the extreme measure of uniforms. The pervasive nineteenth-century understanding that women had a special attachment to clothing (which adversely affected them) probably influenced the gendered Strangite dress regulations. Strangite women could not alter their apparel of their own volition without recrimination.

The Dress Rebellion

One biographer, recognizing the powerful repercussions that can result from taking clothing choices away from women and men, described Strang's 1855 order commanding 'all the women of his kingdom to wear "bloomers" as his 'fatal mistake' (Utley, 1906, p. 306–7). Another historian concurs and suggests that the Mormon dress had much to do with bringing about Strang's 'overthrow' (Leach, 1902). As with most issues and events that occurred on the Strangite Beaver Island, the evidence surrounding women's reactions to the new clothing regulations is conflicting and confusing, with some accounts praising the outfits and others condemning them. Writing to H. A. Chaney in 1877, Wingfield Watson testified that from his observations the Strangite women seemed to 'genuinely like' their Mormon outfits. He also recalled that after Strang's death the women stopped wearing the garment 'with many a regret' (Quaife, 1930, p. 167). Given the persecution women suffered if they did not wear the Mormon dress, it is not surprising that Watson only heard favorable remarks.

Oscar Wetherhold Riegel offered an interesting interpretation of the Mormon dress's introduction on the island. Riegel portrayed Strang as pleased when the women 'accepted the bloomer costume with less objection than he had expected' (1935, p. 242). At the same time, however, he claims that the King was perplexed that most of the women who 'took up the calico bloomers, short skirt and sunbonnet' did so 'as if they were a novelty from Boston or London' (Riegel, 1935, p. 242). In other words, even as Strang attempted to rid his colony of Gentile habits and extravagances, he inadvertently promoted them by introducing what amounted to a new fashion. Intentional or not, according to Riegel, the result was that Strangite women 'wore them and happily' (Riegel, 1935, p. 243). If this was the case, then the Beaver Island women were unique. Almost everyone else in the nineteenth-century United States (from the bloomer costume's most ardent opponents to the women who staunchly wore it all their adult lives) thought the dress was 'ugly' and often said so. Most dress reformers never confused bloomers with fashion. Riegel then made another incredible leap in logic, one that further denigrated the intellect and religious convictions of women. He concluded that 'the men professed to like' the dress and that their praise meant more to the women than 'the pious satisfaction of dressing as the Lord willed' (Riegel, 1935, p. 242-3). Other religions have used clothing as a means of evaluating women's religious commitment and have found women eager to attest to their religiosity with their apparel. So it would seem probable that Strangite women might have also welcomed the opportunity to proclaim their belief in God through their dress.

Although most female Saints wore the Mormon dress, 'King' Strang's command to women to wear short skirts and trousers did not meet with universal approval or compliance. Some women, echoing the opinions of non-Mormon dress reformers, objected to the dress because it was 'ugly' and 'unbecoming.' Others may have used the dress to vent their disapproval of Strang's authoritarian leadership and his position on polygamy. Still others

transactions to January 1, 1849. (1849). Oneida Reserve, New York: Leonard & Company, Printers.

Fitzpatrick, D. C. (1970). *The King Strang story: A vindication of James J. Strang, the Beaver Island mormon*. Lansing, Michigan: National Heritage.

Foster, L. (1981). James J. Strang: The prophet who failed. *Church History, 50*, 182–92.

Foster, L. (1991). *Women, family and utopia: Communal experiments of the shakers, the Oneida community and the Mormons*. Syracuse, NY: Syracuse University Press.

Gates, S. Y. (1930). *The life story of Brigham Young*. New York: Macmillan.

Gilbert, B. (1995). America's only king made Beaver Island his promised land. *Smithsonian, 26*, 84–93.

Hansen, K. (1962). The making of king Strang: A re-examination. *Michigan History, 46*, 201–19.

Joseph, N. (1986). *Uniforms and nonuniforms: Communication through clothing*. Westport, CT: Greenwood Press.

Lauer, J. C., & Lauer, R. H. (1983). Sex roles in nineteenth-century American communal societies.' *Communal Societies, 3*, 16–28.

Leach, M. L. (1903). History of the grand traverse region. *Michigan Historical Collections, 32*, 14–175.

Legler, H. E. (1897). *A Moses for the Mormons: Strang's city of refuge and Island Kingdom*. Milwaukee, WI: Printed for the Parkman Club.

Lewis, D. R. (1983). 'For life, the resurrection and the life everlasting': James J. Strang and Strangite Mormon polygamy, 1849-1856. *Wisconsin Magazine of History, 66*, 274–91.

McDannell, C. (1995). *Material Christianity: Religion and popular culture in America*. New Haven, CT: Yale University Press.

Merritt, Mrs M. A. (1852). *Dress reform practically and physiologically considered*. Buffalo, NY: Jewett, Thomas and Co.

Moore, R. L. (1986). *Religious outsiders and the making of Americans*. New York: Oxford University Press.

Northern Islander. (1851–1856).

Nye, R. B. (1956). *A baker's dozen: Thirteen unusual Americans*. East Lansing: Michigan State University Press.

Pfeiffer, I. (1856). *Lady's second journey round the world*. New York: Harper & Brothers.

Quaife, M. M. (1930). *The kingdom of Saint James: A narrative of the Mormons*. New Haven, CT: Yale University Press.

Quist, J. (1989). Polygamy among James Strang and his followers. *John Whitmer Historical Association Journal, 9*, 31–48.

Riegel, O. W. (1935). *Crown of glory: The life of James J. Strang Moses of the Mormons*. New Haven, CT: Yale University Press.

Roberts, B. H. (1930). *A comprehensive history of the Church of Jesus Christ of Latter Day Saints*. Salt Lake City, UT: Deseret News Press.

Spencer, C. Y., & Harmer, M. (1940). *Brigham Young at home*. Salt Lake City, UT: Deseret Book Company.

Strang, C. J. (1942). Why I am not a Strangite. *Michigan History Magazine, 26.*

Strang, J. J. (1856). *The book of the law of the Lord.* Printed by Command of the King at the Royal Press.

Strang, M. A., (ed.) (1961). *The diary of James J. Strang.* Ann Arbor: Michigan State University Press.

Tinling, M. (1982). Bloomerism comes to California. *California History, 61,* 18–25.

The traverse region, historical and descriptive, with illustrations of scenery and portraits and biographical sketches of some of its prominent men and pioneers. (1884). Chicago, IL: H. R. Page.

Utley, H. M., & Cutheon, B. M. (1906). *Michigan as a province, territory and state, the twenty-sixth member of the federal union.* The Publishing Society of Michigan.

Van Noord, R. (1988). *King of Beaver Island: The life and assassination of James Jesse Strang.* Urbana: University of Illinois Press.

Walkup, F. P. (1947). The sunbonnet woman: Fashions in Utah pioneer costume. *Utah Humanities Review 1.*

Ward, A. N. (1859). *Male life among the Mormons; Or the husband in Utah.* New York: Derby and Jackson.

6

Dress and the Negotiation of Relationships Between the Eastern Dakota and Euroamericans in Nineteenth-Century Minnesota

Sandra Lee Evenson and David J. Trayte

In August 1862, tensions between the Eastern Dakota Indians and Whites erupted in violent conflict. In this bloody watershed in Dakota and White relations, over 450 White men, women and children were killed and approximately 250 were taken captive. The number of Dakota deaths is unknown (Carley, 1976). Accounts of the uprising reveal that perceived cultural orientation was an important factor during the conflict. Dakota individuals who had adopted certain White ways – living in frame or brick houses, farming, practicing Christianity and wearing western-styled dress – were in danger of being treated as Whites, that is, killed or taken captive by the militant Dakota. In many instances, Dakota who dressed like Whites were forced to change back to traditional Dakota dress to save their lives.

It is an understatement to say that the way we look is fundamental to our human interaction. Every day we make sense of others based on how we interpret their dress and appearance.[1] We locate ourselves within our social and cultural environments by dressing the part and we place others within their respective social locations based on our ability to use what we see to identify others as belonging or not belonging to certain groups. Often dress is manipulated to facilitate social interaction, such as dressing for an important interview (Goffman, 1963). The use of dress by the Eastern Dakota between 1834 and 1862 exemplifies the role dress played in the negotiation of relationships between the Dakota and Whites.

Interaction between the Eastern Dakota and Whites dates to the seventeenth century and includes French, British and American traders, the United States military, Protestant missionaries, agents of the Federal government and settlers. The focus of this study is the impact Christian Protestant missionaries had on this dialogue through the ideas they promulgated regarding dress and civilization. Even though Christian missionaries feature prominently in evaluations of the breakdown of Dakota/White relations, along with US Federal agents, they can not be held solely responsible for the final breakdown or subsequent uprising. Rather, Christian missionaries were part of a process that laid the groundwork for what followed.

Theoretical Foundations

Although items of dress, ways of wearing dress and meanings associated with dress vary from culture to culture, there are also commonalities. These include using dress for physical and psychological protection, for personal expression and as an indicator of social location within the social structure, such as gender, economic status, or social role. In the cross-cultural contact situation, the use of dress as a communicator of social position emerges as a common theme. It also appears that individuals who comprise the cultures in contact often manipulate dress as an element in the negotiation of their relationships.

Hay (1992) suggests that clothing styles of the *Luo* people in Western Kenya changed between 1906 and 1936 because of pressure from British missionaries and the growth of a labor market needed for the development of railroads, sisal plantations and dockyards. Missionaries and British administrators exerted pressure on the *Luo* to 'cover themselves,' to wear specific types of garments and to abstain from practices such as scarification. Being a Christian and wearing dress prescribed by British administrators tended to improve *Luo* socioeconomic standing because converts were favored for employment. Hay explores conflicting notions of morality and body exposure between the Luo and the British and the role of Christian converts as cultural innovators. Hay concludes that there are implications of power relations in these dress requirements. The dominant culture was calling the dress tune to which those in the subordinate culture had to dance if they were to survive economically. Similar requirements appeared in other colonial contexts, such as Martin's (1989) study of 'Christians and Clothing in the French Congo, c. 1880-1940,' and Cohn's (1989) and Bean's (1989) explorations of the meaning of clothing in the interaction between the British and the Indians in nineteenth-century India.

In non-colonial interaction between missionaries and indigenous people, Arthur (1997) describes the process of adoption and incorporation of a western item of dress into Hawaiian culture. The *holoku* originated when Hawaiian royalty admired the dresses worn by missionary women, who gladly adapted the style of the day to Hawaiian figures and climate in an effort to encourage western notions of modesty. Because missionaries demanded that less-revealing clothing be worn by women visiting the mission, many Hawaiian visitors wore *holoku* at the mission, but changed back into traditional dress on their return to the village. Missionaries viewed this switching back and forth as a lack of commitment to modesty, but to Hawaiians it was a fulfillment of traditional clothing rules related to appropriateness of dress for time and place. Switching back and forth emerges as a common theme in Eastern Dakota and White relations, as well.

Von Ehrenfels (1979) provides a more general discussion of the role of dress in the 'abuse of power' in colonial interaction. He argues that in early colonial expansion and contact with native (sic) peoples, Europeans did not at first impose European ways, or their dress. Instead, the Europeans tended to adopt the local dress because it was more practical and functional. In the early stages of contact, the people of both cultures act as donors and adopters of goods and ideas. This reciprocity changes as a great European military and civilian presence becomes established in the colonized region. Pressure is exerted on the indigenous people to adopt customs and dress of the imperial power. As more civilians arrive, pressure increases to 'cover up' and appear 'decently dressed.' With increased contact between the colonized and the colonizers, European dress is adopted and functions as an element in the social, political and economic relations that comprise the contact situation.

Erving Goffman's (1959, 1963) approach to understanding the role of the body and by extension the dressed body, in social interaction is characterized by three main features. First, because humans have the ability to control and change the way they look, the body and dress can be used as a resource. By dressing the part, we can manipulate social situations to our benefit. Second, when we dress the part, we locate ourselves within our social and cultural environments and we place others within their respective social locations based on our ability to use what we see to identify others. In this event, dress is used as a form of non-verbal communication and forms a shared vocabulary. Third, by using dress to successfully play a role, we recognize that we have both a personal and a social identity. Every time we dress, we are asking ourselves, often unconsciously, 'Who am I?' and 'Who do I wish to be seen to be?'

The process Von Ehrenfels describes and the role dress plays in it can be seen in the ongoing relationships between the Eastern Dakota and

Euroamericans in Minnesota between 1834 and 1862. There is a large body of literature on Native American culture change resulting from contact with Euroamericans and some of the most telling descriptions of dress and culture change can be found in the papers of Protestant missionaries.

Methodology and Sources

The majority of the documents employed in this study are held in the Minnesota Historical Society archive. These include narratives of trade and exploration, Federal documents, Indian agent papers, missionary papers, popular literature, oral histories, newspaper accounts and photographs. Others, particularly the narratives of exploration, are in the holdings of the O. M. Wilson Library at the University of Minnesota.

The collection of missionary papers, Federal documents and Indian agent literature is voluminous. Examination of the seventy-one collections of missionary documents in the holdings of the Minnesota Historical Society was narrowed to only those seventeen that related to missionaries active in Minnesota prior to the Dakota Conflict of 1862. Of these seventeen, the four most prolific missionary writers were selected for detailed examination. Reverend Doctor Thomas Williamson, Reverend Stephen Riggs and the brothers and lay preachers Samuel and Gideon Pond were actively involved in missionary work in Minnesota throughout the time frame of the study and had a long association with the Dakota people and their lifeways.

The Eastern Dakota

The Eastern Dakota, sometimes referred to as the *Santee* Sioux, lived in the upper Mississippi valley and along the length of the Minnesota River as it stretches to what is today known as South Dakota in the United States.[2] They are the Eastern segment of the Dakota Nation that also includes the *Yankton, Yanktonais* and *Teton* Dakota. The Eastern Dakota comprised four groups: *Mdewakanton, Sisseton, Wahpeton* and *Wahpekute* (Woolworth and Woolworth, 1980).

The Dakota lived by hunting and gathering in the woodlands and river valleys of the upper Mississippi region and on the plains to the west and southwest in what is today Minnesota, Northern Iowa and Eastern South Dakota. Although Dakota women did plant gardens, they were not an agricultural people. Hunting, however, was a communal endeavor. Men did the bulk of the hunting while women established and maintained temporary hunting camps, processed game and gathered and processed fish, berries, roots and other food resources. When the area was hunted-out, the camp was moved to a new area and the process began again (Woolworth and Woolworth, 1980). Prior to the 1830s, buffalo hunting was a fundamental subsistence activity; however, buffalo herds declined precipitously throughout the 1800s. It has been estimated that in 1800 there were approximately 40 million buffalo. By 1865 there were only 15 million buffalo and they were dispersed over a vast region, much of which was not accessible to Eastern Dakota hunters (Thornton, 1987).

Between the time of first contact with Whites in 1660 and the early 1800s, Dakota subsistence patterns remained fairly consistent; however, important changes developed throughout this period. The primary change was Dakota participation in the fur trade industry and their increasing use of and reliance on material goods traded by French and British traders. The establishment of kinship, fictive or real, was crucial to trade and interaction between Eastern Dakota and Whites. Begun by French voyageurs, the practice of marrying Dakota women was continued by British and American traders. The taking of a 'country wife' assured that a trader would have claim to the furs supplied by Dakota hunters who became his relatives (Van Kirk, 1980). In turn, Whites who entered into kinship relations with the Dakota were equally obligated to their Dakota kin.

Following the American revolution in 1776 and territorial negotiations held in Paris in 1783, the land east of the Mississippi River occupied by the Dakota fell within the boundaries of the land claimed by the newly formed United States of America. The Dakota lands in their entirety were eventually claimed by the Americans in 1803 with the purchase of the territory west of the Mississippi River from France. In 1821 Lawrence Taliaferro was posted to Minnesota territory as an 'Indian Agent.' The job of an Indian agent was to control inter-tribal warfare between groups such as the Dakota, Chippewa, Sac and Fox. Peace would facilitate trade, secure the allegiance of the Eastern Dakota to the U. S. Government and 'move (the Dakota) toward civilization' (Taliaferro, 1825, Vol. 7). The agency system was to have significant impact on the Dakota, as the Americans eventually wanted not only trade with the Dakota, but also to settle the region (Meyer, 1967). Settlements by white farmers were viewed as not only a right but an obligation by many citizens of the United States. In 1845, the term Manifest Destiny was coined to express the expansionist spirit of the early 1800s (Goetzmann, 1966). In the *United States Magazine and Democratic Review*, John L. O' Sullivan referred to 'our manifest (read 'obvious') destiny to overspread the continent' (Garraty, 1989, p. 8).

Sandra Lee Evenson and David J. Trayte

Welcoming of Christian Missionaries into Dakota Territory

The primary goal of the Protestant missionaries who arrived in 1834 was the propagation of the Gospel among the Indians. Founded in 1810, the American Board of Commissioners for Foreign Missions, which was responsible for sending missionaries to the Dakota, stated this aim in its constitution. In addition, missionaries had the overt goal of transforming Dakota culture and a fundamental element in this was the transformation of Dakota appearance. In their writings, missionaries such as Samuel and Gideon Pond, who were lay preachers, Reverend Stephen R. Riggs and Reverend Doctor Thomas S. Williamson refer to this in their writings and journals (Riggs, 1869; Williamson, 1875).

The Protestant missionaries could not have arrived at a better time for at least three reasons. First, the 1830s was a time of powerful Christian evangelism (Berkhofer, 1965). The command of Jesus Christ to 'Go into all the world and preach the Gospel to the whole creation' was taken to heart because 'He who believes and is baptized will be saved; but he who does not believe will be condemned' (Mark 16: 15, 16). Missionaries scattered the globe with support from their home churches and newly created mission boards to win the 'heathen' for Christ.

Second, a history of contact with Whites had familiarized the Dakota with White ways and facilitated Dakota acceptance of missionaries into the region. In addition, the kinship ties created between the Dakota women and White trappers and traders introduced individuals of mixed Indian/White parentage into the social, political and economic equation. Because these individuals were bicultural and readily able to incorporate White ways into Dakota life, they often acted as mediators between the Whites and Dakota. Mixed-bloods emerged as a pragmatic people, open to new interpretations of traditional Dakota reciprocity.

Third, by the 1820s, the Dakota were experiencing significant economic difficulties. When Fort Snelling was established in 1819 at the confluence of the Mississippi and Minnesota Rivers, the Dakota welcomed it as a source of goods and services and as a promise of continued trade, kinship and benevolence between Dakota and White Americans (Anderson, 1984). As the early nineteenth century progressed, soldiers and White settlers moved into the territory in ever increasing numbers. As game decreased, the Dakota, Federal agents and the military were faced with the problem of securing a replacement economy for the Dakota. Joseph Renville's invitation to the missionaries provides an illustration.

Renville's father was a French Canadian voyageur and his mother was a Dakota woman from the *Kaposia* band headed by Little Crow, who led the

Dakota Conflict of 1862 (Ackerman, 1931). Through his extensive kinship relations with the Dakota and his astute skills as a trader, Renville had built a highly successful trading operation and bicultural community called *Lac qui Parle*, located 100 miles up the Minnesota River from Fort Snelling. As a result of the depletion of game in the region, Renville's community began to experience economic difficulties (Sibley, 1835). Anderson (1984) suggests that it was the changing economic situation at *Lac qui Parle* that led Renville to invite missionaries to join his community, bringing with them the benefits of Euroamerican culture. It is likely that Renville saw that the Dakota needed to devise strategies to deal with the Euroamericans and changing economic conditions. Enlisting the help of missionaries, with their sources of goods, expertise in agriculture and education and, in the case of the Rev. Dr Williamson, their medical skills, was a reasonable strategy for Renville to adopt. Thus, it was at this juncture in Dakota/White relations that the reciprocal element of Dakota social life gained a greater pragmatism that went beyond kinship obligations. The Eastern Dakota, especially mixed-bloods, welcomed missionaries into their midst for economic survival and were willing to learn the ways of Whites in exchange.

Dakota and Euroamerican Dress, 1830–1850

Samuel and Gideon Pond arrived at Fort Snelling in 1834 and they accepted an offer by agent Taliaferro to establish a settlement twelve miles northwest of the fort near Lake Calhoun (Taliaferro, 1834). Taliaferro had become acutely aware of the depletion of game in the region and the needy state of the Dakota. He provided building materials and farm implements and by the fall of 1834, the Pond brothers were preaching and teaching farming to the *Mdewakantan*.

The Ponds' ethnographic information on the Dakota was obtained over many years (1834–1851) of association with them. Samuel's descriptions provide a clear and detailed picture of Dakota dress. One description of Dakota women's dress is worth presenting in total:

> The entire dress of the Dakota female consisted of a coat, skirt, leggings, moccasins and blanket. The coat of a woman was made of about two yards of printed cotton cloth. The sleeves were tight and it was fitted closely to the body, but was sewn up only an inch or two on the breast, the neck being bare and the coat open at the lower end. The skirt was made of a single piece of blue broad-cloth, the ends being lapped and sewed together, but not across the whole breadth. It was supported at the waist by a girdle, the cloth being doubled under the sash, the outer fold not hanging so low as the inner one. By changing the length of the outer fold, this

skirt might be shortened or lengthened to suit the taste or necessity of the wearer. The skirt was worn smooth in front and behind, but was gathered at the sides. The lower end reached about half way from the knee to the ankle, but was often lower than that; and when the wearer was walking in deep snow, or through grass and bushes, it was worn shorter (Pond, 1986, p. 31–32).

Dakota women wore earrings and often many strands of beads around their necks. Their hair was braided and hung behind their ears and down over their breasts (see Figure 6.1). They used little paint, but did use vermilion pigment on their hair part and as two small dots on their cheeks. Their blankets and other garments, were often embellished with silk ribbons of many colors, embroidery, beadwork and metal ornaments (Pond, 1986).

Pond describes Dakota male dress as being 'well suited' to their lifestyles. Dakota men sometimes went bare-chested or wore cotton shirts in the summer. In winter, they wore coats made of blankets (called capotes) which reached to the knees over these shirts. Their leggings, made of skin or trade cloth, went from ankle to thigh and were tied to their belts with straps. The lower ends fitted smoothly over the moccasin and were secured with the stirrup technique. A breech clout of blue woolen fabric one foot wide and three to four feet long covered the genitals. Thus, the leggings were not attached to the breech clout and they could easily be removed for comfort or necessity, leaving the breech clout in place. Men frequently painted their skins with locally available pigments for hunting and ritual purposes. Their hair was cut across their foreheads but hung long at the sides and back, sometimes in braids (Pond, 1986). (see Figure 6.2).

The blanket was an important feature of Dakota dress for both men and women. Strictly speaking, it might not be considered traditional Dakota dress because it was introduced through trade. However, its introduction in the early eighteenth century and its use by the Dakota transformed the blanket from a novel trade item into quintessentially Indian dress. In many instances blankets and other trade cloths, were used in the same manner that skins had been used, as well as worn folded around the torso. By the 1850s, the term 'blanket Indian' became a well-known phrase employed to refer to 'traditional Indianness.'

White dress and Dakota dress were significantly different in terms of the elements involved and in the total ensemble. Euroamerican male dress from roughly 1830 to 1850 tended to reflect a feminine silhouette, at least in the case of 'fashionable' dress. The waist was nipped in, the shoulders and chest were accentuated and the trousers were worn tight. Coats and decorative waistcoats, cravats tied in various ways and cloth trousers, were standard attire. White linen or cotton dress shirts were fitted with detachable collars

Figure 6.1. Sioux woman, ca. 1870. Photo by Illingworth. Courtesy of the Minnesota Historical Society.

that could be changed throughout the day as they became soiled. Hard-soled shoes or boots were worn with cloth socks. Men selected from a variety of hats, including derbies, broad-brimmed felt hats, straw plantation-style hats and top hats (McClellen, 1969).

Euroamerican women of the period wore full skirts and fitted bodices over linen or cotton undergarments. Foundation garments were worn; however, it is likely that women on the Minnesota frontier dispensed with their corsets. Fashionable dress was very elaborate, with trimmings, lace collars and cuffs, varied sleeve styles, overskirts and decorative aprons. Cashmere and merino shawls, capes and mantles were common elements of female dress (Anderson and Toren, 1984). Hard-soled leather boots and hats and bonnets protected ladies from the elements; a true lady did not have the tanned skin of a woman who worked in the out-of-doors. The hair was worn high and back from the face. Necklines were high and modest. In essence, women's dress of the period was similar to men's dress: even though the cut emphasized the shape of a

Figure 6.2. Sioux uprising leader, Big Eagle (*Waumacetanka*), ca. 1863. Photo by Simon & Shepherd. Courtesy of the Minnesota Historical Society.

man's or woman's body, the body itself was completely covered, with only the hands and face exposed.

The actual dress of men and women going about their daily lives would have varied a great deal within this cursory description, especially on the frontier. Frontier dress tended to be coarser and simpler in materials and quality than dress found in the more settled areas, but it still conveyed the Euroamerican Christian standard of modesty and hygiene. Christian missionaries brought with them not just this standard, but an emphasis on the values related to this standard as an outward manifestation of Christianity and civilization.

Missionary Attempts to Civilize the Dakota Through Dress

On the surface, the goal of the missionaries to spread the Gospel and convert the Dakota to Christianity were clear cut and easily enough stated; but, the methods for accomplishing them were unclear. A debate of the 'chicken or the egg' variety existed among the missionary societies as to whether Indians could receive the 'light of Salvation' simply by being presented with Biblical revelations, or whether fundamental changes in Indian culture were necessary before they were able to 'see the light.' The essential debate became, in other words: Was civilization a prerequisite for salvation, or would salvation lead to civilization? The rigorous efforts of missionaries to change Dakota culture suggests that many missionaries believed that transforming Indian life ways was a prelude to, or at least went hand in hand with, bringing the Dakota to Christ.

As missionaries set to work, they began to push for changes in many fundamental Dakota cultural practices. They wanted the Dakota to abandon communal living and sharing, to give up the chase, to renounce traditional Dakota religion and embrace Christianity, to practice monogamy and in short, to live by the values and patterns of behavior characteristic of Euroamerican civilization. In the missionary literature, the transformation of Dakota dress appears as a stated expectation and goal towards this end. The missionaries, like the majority of their contemporaries, did not separate their goal of bringing the Dakota to Christ from attempting to transform all aspects of Dakota culture.

The approach of Reverend Riggs exemplifies this belief. Riggs believed that converting Dakota women was easier than converting men for two reasons. First, he believed Dakota women held a lower status in Dakota society and Dakota men appeared to be unconcerned about the religious affiliation of their women. Second, Dakota men were required to make more dramatic changes in their cultural patterns, especially in their dress, in order to become Christians than were Dakota women. Pond's description of Dakota female dress was certainly different from prevailing Euroamerican female fashion of the mid-nineteenth century, but was equally modest. By contrast, Dakota men's dress was not modest by Euroamerican standards. Dakota men had long hair, they wore breech clouts which revealed the thigh, they often went bare-chested and painted their skins. In the eyes of the Protestant missionaries, this simply did not constitute the dress of a godly man. Riggs states:

... while the internal change wrought by the Holy Spirit in the heart must be much the same, whether in man or woman, the external change required in the former was not only different but greater in the latter. The woman works already. It will not damage her to keep her house and her person and her children neater than when she was a pagan. **There seemed to be no absolute necessity that she should change the fashion of her dress. It was not unseemly. Rather was it convenient and economical** ... If, however, a Dakota man became Christian, he must not only abandon his ancestral faith, which bound him more closely than the women, for the very reason he was a man and had been inducted into manhood through ceremonies of his religion and must give up his liberty to have more wives than one; **but it very soon came to be understood that the new doctrine required him to cut off his long hair and to change his style of dress, which was not decent** and to go to work like a civilized and Christian man. (emphasis added) (Riggs, 1869, p. 178)

The missionaries considered this disparity in dress to be so great that from the beginning they focused on reforming the dress of Dakota men (Williamson, 1875). What is important is that White dress was decidedly not Dakota dress; and as more and more Euroamericans settled in Minnesota, White dress became the standard against which Dakota dress was measured by the increasingly dominant non-Native population. As a region develops and a new social order emerges, dress, among other things, serves to identify and locate the various groups involved within the emerging social structure (Von Ehrenfels, 1979). In this case, dress became a shared vocabulary in which both Whites and Dakota became versed (Goffman, 1963). Dress was used as a way for both Eastern Dakota and Whites to categorize the Dakota in terms of how willing and able or reluctant and resistant they were to adopt White lifeways.

Riggs' writings are replete with references to the importance of dress as an external symbol of inner change and movement toward Christianity and civilization; however, he was not naïve. He pointed out that a 'change of dress does not change their hearts, but in their [the Dakota's] estimation it does change their relations to the Dakota religion and customs' (Riggs, 1858). Riggs did not elaborate on what he meant by a change in relations. However, given the importance of dress in providing structure and meaning for religious, secular and cultural events and activities, it is reasonable to suggest that not dressing the part makes it difficult to play the part (Goffman, 1959).

Other examples of the missionaries' attempts to transform Dakota dress fell under the goal of making them self-sufficient in Euroamerican terms. Williamson noted that although the Dakota at the mission at *Lac qui Parle* raised sheep, they did not spin yarn or weave cloth. Riggs mentions that spinning and weaving were soon introduced and that *To-tee-doo-ta-win* (Her

Scarlet House Woman), a woman converted to Christianity, was a 'willing scholar' who spun, knit and wove garments for herself and her household (Riggs, 1869). In his annual report to the American Board of Commissioners for Foreign Missions in 1840, Riggs elaborated on the success of his colleagues, the Huggins family, at *Lac qui Parle*:

> Previous to forwarding our last report something had been done in teaching women to spin and knit. At times during this year they have manifested a noble enthusiasm in this work. Under the care of Mrs and Miss Huggins about twenty have learned to spin. Some have spun enough for a short gown, others enough for two or more and a few have commenced spinning for blankets which they have not yet finished.

> Last autumn Mr Huggins prepared a loom for operation and before the cold weather, four women wove for themselves woolen short gowns. This spring they have commenced the manufacture of flax. Several men have swingled flax for their wives and daughters to spin, some of which is already made into cloth. We mention these things, small in themselves, because they are the commencement, as we trust, of civilization of this people and because they are an indication that Indian pride, which makes the Dakota men unwilling to do any thing (sic) but hunt and dance and feast and go to war, must finally give way to their desire of bettering their condition (Riggs, 1840 in a letter to David Greene).

Riggs' satisfaction with the introduction of spinning, weaving and knitting was not based on the intrinsic value of these skills. Rather, he saw this activity as a step, albeit small, toward a Christian lifestyle. Inducing Dakota men to manufacture textiles and Dakota women to sew (as if they did not already), knit, spin and weave was essential to Riggs' concept of civilization (Riggs, 1839).

Concern on the part of the missionaries to transform the appearance of the Dakota went beyond textile production and dress. Those who voiced their opinions on the subject often focused on Dakota hygiene in terms of both body and dress. As summarized by Trayte (1995), the missionaries working among the Dakota found many Dakota customs and habits to be offensive, inappropriate and contrary to their conception of social order and correctness. Riggs complained that Dakota women wore their garments until they 'rotted off.' Williamson described in detail garments glossy with dirt and grease which had not been removed for lack of soap (Williamson, 1875). Soap and salvation appear to have been connected in the Euroamerican mind. As Reverend Riggs stated, 'the gospel of soap was indeed a necessary adjunct and outgrowth of the Gospel of Salvation' (Riggs, 1869).

An important effort related to changing the hygiene practices of the Eastern

Dakota was the cutting of men's hair. When a Dakota man agreed to cut his hair and did so, it was seen as a significant act by both Whites and Dakota (Cullen, 1859). What this meant to the individual is more difficult to say because it was made during a time of socioeconomic upheaval. During the first twenty years of missionary activity among the Dakota, the missionaries reported very little progress. However, as the Dakota experienced increasing breakdown of traditional economic, political and social structures in the 1850s, more and more Dakota men agreed to cut their hair, as well as take up farming (Riggs, 1857).

The changes in dress that Riggs was working for were those encouraged by other individuals such as William J. Cullen, the superintendent for Indian Affairs. In the late 1850s, Cullen allegedly cut the hair of sixteen Dakota men and had them dress in Euroamerican clothing. Each individual received two pairs of pants, two coats, two shirts, a shawl and a cap. Further, each was promised a yoke of oxen and a cow. He wanted to dispose of the breech clout, leggings, long hair, paint and nakedness. The financial incentives motivating the Dakota to agree to Cullen's requests are evident. In a later document, Cullen claimed mass hair cuttings of 200 Dakota (Cullen, 1859). Cullen's efforts represent a subtle shift in how the Federal Government would attempt to 'manage' the Dakota. The use of compensation as a reward for external cultural change set a precedent with disastrous ramifications.

The missionaries, although pleased that more Dakota were adopting 'civilized dress,' were not blind to the reasons for this. Riggs did not view a change in dress as a change in heart. Although he viewed the recent successes as 'a great movement,' he was very aware that he himself had been working for years and had only achieved a small number of converts. As soon as the government put resources into the process, combined with the strained economic situation of the Dakota, the numbers of converts increased (Riggs, 1858). Williamson (1859) gave credit to the missionaries for establishing the base upon which agents such as superintendant Cullen were having their success. Williamson referred to the Dakota refusal to convert in the early years, based on the fear that they would die if they renounced the ways of their ancestors. He suggested this fear had proven false.

Regardless of why a Dakota man chose to cut his hair, the act was seen as significant by both Whites and Dakota. Riggs thought it was the most important step he could take and he relates that one Dakota woman cried every time she looked at her husband's shorn head (Riggs, 1857). Others considered the cutting of hair as an initiation into the 'first degree of civilization' (*The Minnesota Statesman,* 1859, p. 2). After all, many elements of dress can be changed easily from day to day, but cutting one's hair is less easily reversed.

to Euroamericans a willingness to accept what was, by Christian Euro-american standards, clearly a better lifestyle (Goffman, 1963).

By contrast, other Dakota males resisted acculturation and retained what they viewed as traditional Dakota dress. Ironically, this dress included the blanket, originally a trade good introduced by Whites. Excluded from favor, their land sold, restricted to reservations and experiencing severe economic decline, militant 'blanket Indians' rose up in 1862 in violent response, in what is now referred to as The Dakota Conflict. In this conflict, dress was used as a badge of cultural identity and political affiliation. More, it facilitated one's safety or dispatch. Dakota individuals made conscious decisions about who they were – and who they wished to be seen to be (Goffman, 1959).

The role of dress throughout the sequence of contact between the Eastern Dakota and Euroamericans was flexible. It was used differently by individuals within each culture. Euroamericans encouraged adoption of Western dress as a means to civilize the native population, thereby rendering the Dakota controllable, predictable and invisible. The Dakota employed dress as a mechanism for economic and physical survival and as a symbol of cultural allegiance and resistance to assimilation. As economic and political forces changed throughout the early to middle nineteenth century, dress and its meanings were negotiated on an ongoing basis in the context of interaction.

Notes

1. In this study, dress is defined as modifications of the body and supplements to the body. This definition takes into account all products and processes that alter or add to the body. This includes a wide range of modifications such as washing, tattooing, painting, scarring and oiling, as well as supplements such as clothing, jewelry, hair pieces, briefcases and eye glasses (Roach-Higgins and Eicher, 1992).

2. The term Sioux is derived from the Chippewa word for small adder or snake, which the French garbled. The term Sioux is not used by the Dakota as a self-reference; however, common parlance ignores this and employs the word. The term Dakota is used to describe the broad cultural grouping that includes the Eastern Dakota, the Yankton, the Yanktonais and the Teton Dakota. The terms Whites and Euroamericans are used to refer to non-Native Americans who were in contact with the Eastern Dakota.

References

Ackerman, G. W. (1931). Joseph Renville of Lac qui Parle. *Minnesota History*, 12, 231–46.

Anderson, G. C. (1984). *Kinsmen of another kind*. Lincoln, NE: University of Nebraska Press.

Anderson, M. G. & Toren, H. (1984). Wrapped in style. *Minnesota History, 49,* 57–64.

Anderson, G. C. & Woolworth, A. R. (Eds.). (1988). *Through Dakota eyes: Narrative accounts of the Minnesota Indian War of 1862.* St. Paul, MN: Minnesota Historical Society Press.

Arthur, L. B. (1997). Cultural authentication refined: The case of the Hawaiian holoku. *Clothing and Textiles Research Journal, 15 (3),* 129–139.

Bean, S. S. (1989). Gandhi and khadi, the fabric of Indian independence. In A. B. Weiner & J. Schneider (Eds.), *Cloth and human experience* (pp. 355–76). Washington DC: Smithsonian Institution Press.

Berkhofer, R. F. Jr. (1965). *Salvation and the savage: An analysis of Protestant missions and American Indian response, 1787–1862.* City not given: University of Kentucky Press.

Brown, S. J. (1897, April & May). In captivity: The experience, privations and dangers of Sam'l J. Brown and others, while prisoners of the hostile Sioux, during the massacre and war of 1862. *Mankato Weekly Review.* St. Paul, MN: Minnesota Historical Society Collections.

Carley, K. (1976). *The Sioux uprising of 1862.* St. Paul, MN: The Minnesota Historical Society.

Cohn, B. S. (1989). Cloth, clothes and colonialism: Indian in the nineteenth century. In A. B. Weiner & J. Schneider (Eds.), *Cloth and human experience* (pp. 303–53). Washington DC: Smithsonian Institution Press.

Cullen, W. J. (1859). Manuscript letter to A. B. Greenwood, August 13. *National Archives Record Group 75,* LR. St. Peter's Agency. St. Paul, MN: Minnesota Historical Society Collections.

Garraty, J. A. (1989). *1,001 things everyone should know about American history.* New York: Doubleday.

Goetzmann, W. H. (1966). *Exploration and empire: the explorer and the scientist in the winning of the American west.* New York: W. W. Norton & Company.

Goffman, E. (1959). *The presentation of self in everyday life.* Garden City, NJ: Doubleday Anchor Books.

Goffman, E. (1963). *Behavior in public places.* New York: Macmillan Publishing.

Hay, J. (1992). Who wears the pants? Christian missionaries, migrant labor and clothing in colonial Western Kenya. *Discussion Papers in African Humanities, Number 23* (pp. 1–23). Boston: Boston University African Studies Center.

Herd, I. V. D. (1865). *History of the Sioux war and massacres of 1862 and 1863.* New York: Harper & Brothers, Publishers.

Martin, P. (1989). *Christians and clothing in the French Congo, c. 1880–1940.* Paper presented at the meeting of the African Studies Association.

McClellen, E. (1969). *History of American costume, 1607–1870.* New York: Tudor Publishing Company.

Meyer, R. W. (1967). *History of the Santee Sioux: United States Indian Policy on Trial.* Lincoln, NE: University of Nebraska Press.

Myrick, N. et. al. vs. The United States, for goods and supplies furnished the Sioux Indians at upper and lower agencies in Minnesota between 1st day of June, 1861 and the outbreak of said Indians in August, 1862. *Special Files of the Office of Indian Affairs, 1807–1904.* NARG 75. St. Paul, MN: Minnesota Historical Society Collections.

Pond, S. W. (1842). Manuscript letter to D. C. Green, May 10. *American Board of Commissioners for foreign missions.* St. Paul, MN: Minnesota Historical Society Collections.

Pond, S. W. (1986). *The Dakota or Sioux in Minnesota as they were in 1834.* St. Paul, MN: The Minnesota Historical Society.

Riggs, S. (1839). Letter to the *Missionary Herald*, March 26. St. Paul, MN: Minnesota Historical Society Collections.

Riggs, S. (1840). Manuscript letter to David Greene. *Annual report of the Lac qui Parle mission.* St. Paul, MN: Minnesota Historical Society Collections.

Riggs, S. (1857). Letter to the *St. Paul Advertiser*, March 31. St. Paul, MN: Minnesota Historical Society.

Riggs, S. (1858). Manuscript letter to J. M. Gordon. St. Paul, MN: Minnesota Historical Society Collections.

Riggs, S. (1869). *Tahkoo Wahkan; or The Gospel Among the Dakotas.* Boston: Congregational Sabbath-School and Publishing Society.

Roach-Higgins, M. E. & Eicher, J. B. (1992). Dress and identity. *Clothing and Textiles Research Journal, 10 (4),* 1–8.

Sibley, H. H. (1835). Manuscript letter to Ramsey Crooks, April 29. *American Fur Company Papers.* St. Paul, MN: Minnesota Historical Society Collections.

Sisseton and Bands of Sioux Indians vs. The United States, No. 22524 (1901–1907). *Court Claims of the United States.* St. Paul, MN: Minnesota Historical Society.

Taliaferro, L. (1825). *Manuscript journal, 7.* St. Paul, MN: Minnesota Historical Society Collections.

Taliaferro, L. (1834*). Manuscript journal, July 7.* St. Paul, MN: Minnesota Historical Society Collections.

The Minnesota Statesman (1859). Editorial, July 29. St. Paul, MN: Minnesota Historical Society Collections.

Thornton, R. (1987). *American Indian holocaust and survival: A population history since 1492.* Norman, OK: University of Oklahoma Press.

Trayte, D. (1995). The gospel of soap. In M. E. Roach-Higgins, J. B. Eicher and K. K. P. Johnson (Eds.), *Dress and identity* (pp. 293–98). New York: Fairchild Publications.

Van Kirk, s. (1980). *'Many tender ties:' Women in fur-trade society in western Canada, 1670–1870.* Winnipeg, Manitoba: Watson & Dwyer Publishing Ltd.

Von Ehrenfels, U. R. (1979). Clothing and power abuse. In J. M. Cordwell and R. A. Schwartz (Eds.), *The fabrics of culture* (pp. 399–403). The Hague: Mouton Publishers.

Williamson, T. S. (1859). Manuscript letter to S. B. Treat, November 18. *American*

Board of Commissioners for foreign missions. St. Paul, MN: Minnesota Historical Society Collections.

Williamson, T. S. (1875, November). Dakota women. *Iape oave (The word carrier)*, *4 (11)*, 44.

Woolworth, A. R. and Woolworth, N. L. (1980). Eastern Dakota settlement and subsistence patterns prior to 1851. *Minnesota Archeologist, 39*, 71–89.

that no institution has played a more important role in social cohesion in the black community. The church gave birth to schools, banks, insurance companies and low-income housing. It provides an arena for political activities and nurtures young talent for various forms of artistic development. The Black Church serves as an avenue for the power and prestige otherwise denied blacks in society and also serves to create a sense of ethnic community and ethnic identity (Clark, 1965, 1989: Drake and Clayton, 1962; Toulis, 1997; William, 1996). Much of black culture is indebted to the black religious tradition. Thus, '[a] demise of the black religious tradition would have profound implications for the preservation of black culture.' (Lincoln and Mamiya, 1990, p. 10). On the other hand, the institution lauded for its strength and source of power is also criticized as a stumbling block to assimilation and as a form of voluntary isolation (Clark, 1965, 1989; Frazier, 1964; Orum, 1966; Silberman, 1964).

Today, seven major denominations make up the dominant body of The Black Church: African Methodist Episcopal; African Methodist Episcopal Zion; Christian Methodist Episcopal; National Baptist Convention, USA Incorporated; National Baptist Convention of America Unincorporated; Progressive National Baptist convention; and the Church of God in Christ. Researchers (Lincoln and Mamiya, 1990; Roof and McKinney, 1987; Walker, 1981) estimate that more than 80 percent of all Black Christians are in these seven denominations, with smaller communions accounting for an additional six percent. The churches composing these denominations are best described by Lincoln and Mamiya's (1990) dialectical model. This model holds that African American churches are institutions that are involved in a constant series of dialectical tensions that must be understood in order to obtain a holistic picture. There are six pairs of dialectically related polar opposites that give a comprehensive view of the complexity of these churches as social institutions, including their roles and functions in African American communities. The six main pairs of related polar opposites are the dialectic between (a) priestly and prophetic function, (b) other-worldly versus this-worldly, (c) universalism and particularism, (d) communal and privatistic, (e) charismatic versus bureaucratic and (f) resistance versus accommodation. This model allows churches to be viewed along a continuum of dialectical tensions and constant interactions and helps to prevent stereotyping African American churches into rigid categories.

The Black Church has served and continues to serve as a source of power in the African American community. Lincoln (1974) noted that:

There is no disjunction between the Black Church and the Black community. The church is the spiritual face of the Black community and whether one is a 'church member' or not is beside the point in any assessment of the importance and meaning of the Black Church. Because of the peculiar nature of the Black experience and the centrality of institutionalized religion in the development of that experience, the time was when the personal dignity of the Black individual was communicated almost entirely through his church affiliation. . . . The church still accepts a broad-gauge responsibility for the black community inside and outside its formal communion. (p. 115–6).

The Black Church today is most commonly referred to as the African American Church. Despite the pluralism and the plurality of views that exist in African American churches and communities, the church still accepts a broad-gage responsibility for the African American community. Also, wherever people of the African diaspora are gathered in significant enough numbers, a qualitatively different cultural form of expressing Christianity is found, regardless of denomination (Lincoln and Mamiya, 1990; Paris, 1985; Sobel, 1979; Toulis, 1997). In addition to the differences in degrees of social assimilation and social class differentiation, the church continues to be a refuge for African Americans in a hostile world.

The Sacred Cosmos and Religion

The black sacred cosmos is dominated by the Christian God, which is ultimately revealed in Jesus of Nazareth. African American Christians hold to the same orthodox beliefs as that of white Christians, but place different degrees of emphasis and salience to certain particular theological views. In addition, during slavery and the postbellum period, Christianity was not necessarily used by Blacks as it was delivered by white racists. In the experience of suffering and struggle, its truth was authenticated and produced an indigenous faith that emphasized dignity, freedom and human welfare (Cone, 1986; Lincoln & Mamiya, 1990; Wilmore, 1983).

In The Black Church, emphasis is historically placed on the Old Testament notion of God as an avenging, conquering, liberating God. A direct relationship between the Holocaust of slavery and the notion of divine rescue is found in the theological perceptions of African American laity and the themes of their preaching (Cone, 1986). Also, greater weight is given to the biblical views of the importance of human personality and human equality implicit in the notion of all human being as 'children of God.' This emphasis is directly related to the struggle of African Americans to affirm and establish their humanity and their worth as persons (Cone, 1986; Cunningham, 1985; Lincoln and Mamiya, 1990; Mitchell, 1975; Wilmore, 1983).

The superlative value of the sacred cosmos is 'freedom' (Lincoln and Mamiya, 1990, p. 5). The implication of freedom has differed depending upon the time and the context. During slavery it meant release from bondage; after emancipation it meant the right to be educated, employed and mobile. In the twentieth century it means social, political and economic justice. Regardless of the period, ' freedom has always meant the absence of any restraint which might compromise one's responsibility to God' (Lincoln and Mamiya, 1990, p. 4). Because of the failure of white religionists to relate the gospel of Jesus to the pain of being black in a white racist society, a black theology of liberation appeared (see Cone, 1986) and pervades the preaching of African Americans even in the late twentieth century.

The search for transcendence – an enduring fellowship with God which placed its communicants beyond the confines of the burdens of everyday life – is another element of the sacred cosmos and is possibly the element closest to African cosmology. Olupona (1991) indicated that the issues of transcendence and the sacred are salient in African traditional religion and ordinary human experiences mimic transcendence and the sacred. Both traditional and contemporary African religion is an experiential phenomenon; the experience of God is one in which the sacred and the profane tend to be symmetrical. Because the worship setting provides the occasion for particular periods of intimacy characterized by intense enthusiasm and open display of emotions (Daniel, 1942; DuBois, 1903; Lincoln and Mamiya, 1990; Mydral, 1944), this element has been condemned as extreme emotionalism and ascribed to the 'animal nature' of Africans and African descendants (Moore, 1981; Mydral, 1944). However, Daniel (1942) indicated that the social nature of those who commonly seek transcendence (i.e. an ecstatic experience) prevents the type of isolation that accompanies inferiority and moves one to a level where he or she can live above the handicap of everyday life. In the churches of upper-class African Americans, less emotionalism is found because of their adjustment to life's demands and the reduced need to seek escape through emotional release. Consensus, however, has never been reached with relation to the issue of emotionalism in the church.

Notwithstanding the pluralism and plurality of The Black Church, the resulting theology is one of liberation and survival and its frame of reference is the condition of the community out of which it arises (Cone, 1986). It seeks to interpret the theological significance of the being of a community whose existence is threatened by the power of non-being (Cone, 1986, p. 16). The sources of the theology are the African American experience, history, culture, the revelation of God at work today, Scripture, and Christian traditions of the Black Church. It seeks to create a theological norm in harmony with the condition of African Americans and Biblical revelation that relates itself to the human condition and the manifestation of Jesus necessary for black liberation.

While the sacred cosmos described dominates The Black Church, it too must be considered in light of the complexity of the dialectical model put forth by Lincoln and Mamiya (1990). Thus, a theological tension exists and interacts with the socio-political variables confronting any congregation. The most apparent feature of the sacred cosmos is its practicality in the lives of African American people.

Disagreement is found in the scholarly and theological literature relative to the African roots or West African religious influences in The Black Church. African religious scholars have recently documented similarities in African traditional religions in general and specifically how those traditions are still found in contemporary African religion. Also, Mulago (1991) has presented correspondence between traditional black African religions and Christianity. He noted that traditional black African religion consists of a complex of ideas, feelings and rites based on belief (a) in two worlds, visible and invisible, (b) that both worlds involve community and hierarchy, (c) in the intersection of the two worlds and (d) in a Supreme Being, Creator and Father of all that exists. Utmost importance is placed on the common belief of a Supreme Being who is the original source of life and of all resources of life. Oosthuizen (1991) also noted the correspondence between religious activities in the contemporary South African church and the contemporary African American church. He noted that [worship experiences] are not something one sits through, but are dynamic and related to specific needs in the religious context which involves meeting the needs of the flock.

The general consensus is that the influence of traditional African religion is evident in the life of African Americans. Wilmore (1983) noted that the traditional religions of Africa have a single overarching characteristic that survived in a diluted form – 'a powerful belief that the individual and the community were continuously involved with the spirit world in the practical affairs of daily life' (p. 15). He argued that African religions know nothing of a rigid demarcation between the natural and the supernatural or between secular and sacred activities. Others (e.g. Farajaje-Jones, 1990; Rawick, 1972) agree and suggest that in the life of African Americans, religion is not something apart from the rest of existence but its source.

One might conclude, then, that the sacred cosmos of The Black Church and thus, the African American community and culture, is rooted in Africa. If The Black Church serves as the primary cultural and social institution in the African American community, as the cultural and spiritual link to the ancestors, as well as the repository for cultural memory, dress in the African American church must also reflect this influence.

that "I may be financially poor, but I'm culturally rich"' (William, 1996, p. 11). There is no essential African American church dress.

The Black Church, no doubt, played the primary role in preserving the historical significance of African modalities in dress as it assumed the role of curator of cultural memory for African Americans in general. It is not surprising to find profound expression of culture in the dress of African Americans, nor to find perhaps, the greatest expression in the African American church.

O'Neal (1994, 1997a and in press) has shown that although enslaved Africans were not allowed to bring with them objects of their material culture, their cultural modalities in dress survived the Middle Passage as well as four hundred years of slavery and segregation.[3] African cultural modalities seen today in the dress of African Americans form the basis for an African American aesthetic of dress. The historical significance of such modalities, however, became complex and it is not to be assumed that the African influences are static representations of archaic retentions. Instead, what is seen is a living tradition with African roots and a New World form. These cultural influences were transformed and are continuously adapted to a new place and a new time and are thus transformed.

Impact of the sacred cosmos on dress

In discussing dress, descriptions most often focus on the external body. However, the external/internal dichotomy is an artificial one in the African American context since this context is heavily influenced by African cosmology. In African cosmology, no distinction is made between the body and the self: the body is the self and the self is the body. Because of media representations of blackness and the dominant cultural hegemony, African Americans and other people of color are positioned outside of the norm or as the 'Other.' Such images determine how members of the dominant culture will interact, relate and respond to people. Therefore, African Americans find the self as represented in the body to be stigmatized. The deeply ideological nature of imagery also determines how and what one thinks about the self (Hooks, 1992). As Synnott (1993) and Goffman (1963) contend, those with stigmatized bodies are aware that the body is political and central to identity and survival. Understanding that the stigmatized self is also the marginalized self, ways have been sought to simplify acculturation, i.e. acceptance. Thus, thermal and chemical hair straighteners, products to lighten the skin and educational institutions – which began in 'Negro' churches – instructing students in manners and ways of the dominant culture, serve this end. African Americans are not indifferent to their bodies but develop feelings of love or hate for their bodies because of political and practical reasons.

African Americans have responded, through dress, to the stigmatized and marginalized self in various ways. Hooks (1990) has suggested that persons marginalized may use such status as a base for resistance. Craig (1997) interprets the wearing of the 'conk' along with other feminine forms of dress, by black male subcultures, as a badge of street masculinity and a way of rejecting the dominant culture's hegemonic view of masculinity.[4] Yet, it was not uncommon for such forms of dress to be seen worn by gospel singers in black churches and even some less extreme versions by preachers. A modified version of the 'conk' as well as 'feminine' colors have recently surfaced in the fashions worn by some African American men both in and outside of the church. These styles are simply part of the range of acceptable dress. A problem, then, in the African American community is that of confronting the values of the dominant cultural aesthetics that negate the body, and therefore the self. A central role of religion and The Black Church has been and continues to be that of liberation – i.e. ' the emancipation of black minds and black souls from white definitions of black humanity' (Cone, 1986, p. 29). The African American Church continues to facilitate the search for identity and authenticity of its people and in so doing, serves as the cultural keeper and expositor of African American culture for African American people.

Dress calls attention to the external or social body, but is also a product of material culture. According to Toure (1973), 'Material cultural production and spiritual cultural production are dialectically linked and exercise a reciprocal influence on each other' (p. 6). In African cosmology, distinctions are not made between the visible and invisible worlds. Thus, the form of the biological package, i.e., the body, may be elaborated, distorted, or even denied, to create the other-worldly image as the two worlds interact in ritual or ceremony (Thieme and Eicher, 1990). Perhaps an aspect of the importance of dressing up and the use of the exotic in dress for church, is a transformation of this practice in the search for transcendence.

Evidence presented earlier supports the contention of similarity between the sacred cosmos and the culture in general of African Americans. 'The core values of black culture like freedom, justice, equality, an African heritage and racial parity at all levels of human intercourse, are raised to ultimate levels and legitimated by the black sacred cosmos' (Lincoln and Mamiya, 1990, p. 7). African Americans' approach to dress in the context of the church is a concrete manifestation of these core values. Therefore, dress, in the context of The Black/African American Church in America, can be said to be an authentic representation of African American culture.

Notes

1. The term 'The Black Church' is capitalized in this paper when it is used to reference the collective Black/African American Christian churches in North America. Reference is also made in the paper to the 'slave' church, then the 'Negro' church and finally the 'African American' church. The use of these terms follow an historical progression, and all refer to people of African descent living in the US. 'Black' and 'African American' are sometimes used interchangeably.

2. The US apparel industry has recognized the characteristic differences in the taste of African Americans in apparel. Retailers such as J. C. Penney, Spiegel, Sears and Marshall Field's have begun to include in their merchandise assortments lines to target the aesthetic taste of African Americans.

3. According to Thieme and Eicher (1990), dress in Africa 'includes the aspect of gesture, such as when a garment is manipulated when worn; effects of dress on adornment or posture, gait and freedom or restriction of body movement; and poses or certain physical gestures that must accompany the wearing of artifacts of dress in order that a cultural group views an individual as currently dressed' (p. 4). O'Neal (1977 c) refers to similar 'energy' in dress as the element of *style*.

4. The 'conk' was a style of straightened hair worn by African American male subcultures between the 1940s and the 1960s, which was often combed into a swirl of waves atop the forehead. The style was achieved by 'processing' the hair with a lye-based cream (Craig, 1997, p. 404).

References

Blassingame, J. W. (1972). *The slave community: Plantation life in the antebellum South*. New York: Oxford University Press.

Brown, C. (1971). Black religion – 1968. In H. M. Nelson, R. L. Yokley, & A. K. Nelson (Eds.), *The Black church in America* (pp. 17–28). New York: Basic Books, Inc.

Clark, K. B. (1965/1989) *Dark ghetto: Dilemmas of social power* (2nd. ed.). Middletown, CN: Wesleyan University Press.

Cone, J. H. (1986). *The black theology of liberation* (2nd. ed.) Maryknoll, NY: Orbis Books.

Craig, M. (1997). The decline and fall of the conk; or, how to read a process. *Fashion Theory: The Journal of Dress, Body and Culture, 1 (4)*, 339–52.

Cunningham, F. T. (1985). Wandering in the wilderness: Black Baptist thought after emancipation. *American Baptist Quarterly, 4*, 268–81.

Daniel, V. E. (1942). Ritual and stratification in Chicago Negro churches. *American Sociological Review, 7*, 352–61.

Drake, St. C. & Clayton, H (1962). *Black metropolis* (rev. ed.). New York: Harper & Row.

DuBois, W. E. B. (1903/1969). *The souls of black folk*. New York: The New American Library.

Eicher, J. B., & Roach-Higgins, M. E. (1992). Definition and classification of dress. In R. Barnes & J. B. Eicher (Eds.), *Dress and gender: Making and meaning in cultural context* (pp. 8–20). New York: Berg.

Everett, S. (1991). *History of slavery*. Sacacus, NJ: Cartwell Books, Inc.

Farajaje-Jones, E. (1990). *In search of Zion: The spiritual significance of Africa in Black religious movements*. New York: Peter Lang.

Faust, D. G. (1980). Culture, conflict and community: The meaning of power on an ante-bellum Plantation. *Journal of Social History, 14*, 83–97.

Foster, H. B. (1997). *'New raiments of self': African American clothing in the antebellum South*. Oxford and New York: Berg.

Frazier, E. F. (1964). *The Negro church in America*. New York: Schocken Books.

Goffman, E. (1963). *Stigma: Notes on the management of spoiled identity*. Englewood Cliffs, NJ: Prentice Hall.

Herskovits, M. J (1941*). The myth of the Negro past*. New York: Harper and Row.

Hoebel, E. A. (1965). Clothing and adornment. In M. E. Roach & J. B. Eicher (Eds.). *Dress, adornment and the social order* (15–27). New York: John Wiley & Sons, Inc.

Hooks, B. (1990). *Yearning: Race, gender and cultural politics*. Boston: South End Press.

Hooks, B. (1992). *Black looks race and representation*. Boston: South End Press.

Jones, I. & Holloman, L. O. (1990). The role of clothing in the African American church. In B. Starke, L. O. Holloman and B. Nordquist (Eds.), *African American dress and adornment: A cultural perspective* (69–80). Dubuque, IA: Kendall/Hunt.

Kelley, R. D. G. (1997). Nap time: Historicizing the Afro. *Fashion Theory: The Journal of Dress, Body & Culture, 1 (4)*, 339–52.

Levine, L. W. (1977*). Black culture and black consciousness: Afro-American folk thought from slavery to freedom*. New York: Oxford University Press.

Lincoln, C. E. (1974). *The black church since Frazier*. New York: Schocken Books.

Lincoln, C. E. & Mamiya, L. H. (1990). *The Black Church in the African American experience*. Durham, NC: Duke University Press.

Mbiti, J. S. (1969). *African religions and philosophy*. New York: Praeger.

Mercer, F. (1987). Black hair/Style politics. *New Formations, 3*, 33–54.

Mitchell, H. H. (1975). *Black belief: Folk beliefs of Blacks in America and West Africa*. New York: Harper and Row.

Moore, D. O. (1981). The withdrawal of Blacks from Southern Baptist churches following emancipation. *Baptist History and Heritage, 16*, 12–8.

Mulago, V. (1991). Traditional African religion and Christanity. In J. K. Olupono (Ed.), *African traditional religions in contemporary society* (pp. 119–34). NY: Paragon.

Mydral, G. (1944). *An American dilemma*. New York: Harper & Row Publishers, Inc.

Olupono, J. K (1991). Major issues in the study of African traditional religion. In J.

K. Olupono (Ed.), *African traditional religions in contemporary society* (pp. 25–34). NY: Paragon House.

O'Neal, G. S. (1994). African-American aesthetic of dress: Symmetry through diversity. In M. R. DeLong & A. M. Fiore (Eds.), *Aesthetics of Textiles and Clothing: Advancing multidisciplinary perspectives*. ITAA Special publication #7 (pp. 212–23). Monument, CO.

O'Neal, G. S. (1997a). African-American aesthetic of dress: subcultural meaning and significance. In I. Rauch and G. F. Carr (Eds.), *Semiotics around the world: Synthesis in diversity* (pp. 307–10). New York: Mouton de Gruyter.

O'Neal, G. S. (1997b). *Style as power: On the rejection of the accepted*. Manuscript submitted for publication.

O'Neal, G. S. (1998). African-American women's professional dress as expression of ethnicity. *Journal of Family and Consumer Sciences* 90 (1), 28–33.

O'Neal, G. S. (In press). African-American aesthetic of dress: Part I – Current manifestations. *Clothing and Textile Research Journal*.

Oosthuizen, G. C. (1991). The place of traditional religion in contemporary South Africa. In J. K. Olupona (Ed.), *African traditional religions in contemporary society* (pp. 35–50). New York: Paragon House.

Orum, A. M. (1966). A reappraisal of the social and political participation of Negores. *American Journal of Sociology, 72*, 32–46.

Parrinder, G. (1970). *West African religion*. New York: Barnes & Noble.

Paris, P. J. (1985). *The social teaching of the Black church*. Philadelphia: Fortress Press.

Platt, A. M. (1991). *E. Franklin Frazier Reconsidered*. New Brunswick, NJ: Rutgers University Press.

Raboteau, A. J. (1978). *Slave religion: The 'Invisible Institution' in the antebellum South*. New York: Oxford University Press.

Rawick, G. P. (1972). *From sundown to sunup: The making of the black community*. Westport, CN: Greenwood Publishing Company.

Robinson, A. L. (1994). Plans dat comed from God: Institution building and the emergence of Black leadership in reconstruction Menphis. In D. G. Nieman (Ed.), *Church and community among black southerners 1865–1900* (pp. 85–116). New York & London: Garland Publishing, Inc.

Roof, W. C. & McKinney, W. (1987). *American mainline religion: Its changing shape and future*. New Brunswick, NJ: Rutgers University Press.

Semmes, C. E. (1992). *Cultural hegemony and African American development*. Westport, CN: Prager.

Siberman, C. E. (1994). Crisis in black and white. New York: Random House.

Simkins, A. A. (1990). Function and symbol in hair and headgear among African American women. In B. Starke, L. O. Holloman and B. Nordquist (Eds.), *African American dress and adornment: A cultural perspective* (pp. 69–80). Dubuque, IA: Kendall/Hunt.

Sobel, M. (1979). *Trabelin' On: The slave journey to an Afro-Baptist faith*. Westport, CN: Greenwood.

Synnott, A. (1993). *The body social: Symbolism, self and society*. London and New York: Routledge.

Thieme, O. C. & Eicher, J. B. (1990). African dress: Form, action, meaning. In B. Starke, L. O. Holloman and B. Nordquist (Eds.), African American dress and adornment: A cultural perspective (pp. 69–80). Dubuque, IA: Kendall/Hunt.

Thompson, F. W. (1974). *African art in motion*. Berkley: University of California Press.

Toure, S. (1973). A dialectical approach to culture. In R. Chrisman & N. Hare (Eds.), *Contemporary Black thought* (pp. 3–25). Indianapolis/New York: The Bobbs-Merrill company, Inc.

Toulis, N. R. (1997). *Believing identity: Pentecostalism and the mediation of Jamaican ethnicity and gender in England*. Berg: Oxford and New York.

Walker, D. C. (1981). The Black church in America. *Dollars and Sense, 7 (2)*.

Willett, F. (1993). *African Art*. New York: Thames and Hudson.

William, L. (1996, May 12) In defense of the church hat. *New York Times*, Sec. 13, p. 1, 11.

Wilmore, G. S. (1983). *Black religion and black radicalism: An interpretation of the religious history of Afro-American people* (2nd ed.), New York: Orbis Books.

8

Fashion and Identity of Women Religious

Susan O. Michelman

This chapter focuses on the data of twenty-six Roman Catholic nuns, or as those in non-cloistered orders prefer to be called, women religious, who relinquished religious habits for secular dress. It examines dynamics of personal identity announcements and social identity placements that are not congruous. Prior to the 1960s, women's religious orders were quite homogeneous both in exterior manifestations such as their dress in the habit and in the purpose and spirit that permeated them (Ebaugh, 1977, p. 13). Their personal and social persona were one and the same. The life of a woman religious was highly prescribed and routinized. During the 1960s and 1970s, the majority of women in non-cloistered orders of the Roman Catholic Church, as part of larger reforms dictated by Vatican II in 1962, relinquished religious habits for secular fashions. Many had worn habits for a large portion of their lives, often between twenty and thirty-five years, dressing in them from the moment they arose in the morning until they retired in the evening. Their social identities were more outwardly visible than their personal identities, as they had relinquished individuality for social control of their bodies by the Church. From the time that women religious first wore religious attire as novices, they were instructed to view themselves not as individuals, but as representatives of a group. Their habits symbolized their commitment and vows to the Church which superseded their individual identities (Griffin, 1975).

Prior to Vatican II, which occurred in 1962, for many women in non-cloistered religious orders, the habit came to be viewed in a more negative than positive light. Their perception was that this dress communicated a social identity that inhibited their ability to express personal identities that would allow them to function more fully in secular environments. The habit clearly symbolized their total commitment to their order, but it was described by them as a form of social control in that it affected their ability to interact and communicate freely as individuals. As described by women in this study, the habit made them feel less than fully human.

Ebaugh (1977), in her research on religious orders, confirmed that personal identity issues were not addressed by the Church prior to Vatican II. She describes the indoctrination of women religious as demanding ideological totalism (Lifton, 1961). In her research, she discussed the mechanisms of social control that made totalism work. The symbolic gesture of exchanging secular dress for black religious garb was 'the first symbolic gesture of 'putting off the world and entering into a new life ' (Ebaugh, 1977, p. 21).

> The uniform was characterized by complete simplicity and modesty, being high-necked, long-sleeved and ankle length. In addition to the uniform, feminine lingerie was exchanged for simple white cotton underwear, indicating that the postulant was exchanging her womanly enjoyments for austere dress that would now symbolize her as the spouse of Jesus Christ. In addition, henceforth the woman was no longer to be distinguished by dress from the other women in the institute with whom she would live (Ebaugh, 1977, p. 21–2).

Historically, the habit did not start as a symbol of religious life, rather, it was the widow's dress of the day. In the case of the Sister's of St Joseph, it started with six women in France in the seventeenth century, who went out two by two to minister to the needs of the people (Aherne, 1983). They wore modest black dresses and veils, because women who were widows were allowed more personal freedom than those who were single or married. They could travel without male chaperones. These women were able to circumvent both church and state regulations. This early 'habit' was a protection in a sense and it allowed them to be free to do the work they wanted. Some of the women in this study felt that prior to Vatican II, the Church saw the habit as a protection against the 'evils of the world.' The voluminous layers of black serge and veiling covering their bodies, head and neck cloaked both femininity and sexuality. In the eyes of the women in this study, it also suppressed their personal identity. Ironically, whereas the habit had historically begun as a way of achieving autonomy, dress had evolved into a way of suppressing personal identity, through the social control of their bodies. It is important to bear in mind that the women in this study did not leave religious orders after Vatican II; rather, they had remained as members and had negotiated their identity within the boundaries of the Church. These women religious negotiated some social control issues with the Church symbolically by discarding the habit for secular dress.

The women in my study dress in contemporary fashions that make them indiscernible from any other modestly dressed professional woman in

American society. Some orders like their members to wear some visible indication of their affiliation as women religious, such as a ring or cross (Ebaugh, 1993), but many of the women in my study did not. The habit, for many women in non-cloistered religious orders, came to be viewed by them prior to Vatican II, in a more negative than positive light. Their perception was that dress inhibited their ability to have positive social interactions as people; rather, they were frequently stereotyped by the symbolic nature of the habit. The habit visually symbolized and promoted interactions with others that reinforced this belief.

Interviewer: If you were sitting there in a habit, I would feel differently. I would feel a little more inhibited, more cautious, more formal.

Respondent: Your experience is the other end of what I'm trying to describe to you about coming out of habit.

Interviewer: You are talking about it being an inhibition for you – an inhibition in social interaction?

Respondent: Yes it was – because immediately when people saw us, they didn't see us as the individual that you were. They saw you as the woman religious and they immediately raise you above the human level. We had privilege and prestige and we were considered to be in a holier state of life. That's not true. I've chosen another way to live but it is not a holier way – it's a different way.

Currently, the work and lifestyles of women religious in active orders is highly liberated in contrast to the period prior to Vatican II. When the habit was relinquished, social control of the body by the Church decreased. For example, today, women exhibit a high degree of personal autonomy, many living alone or in small groups instead of orders, fully integrated into the non-celibate lay community (Ebaugh, 1993). Dress, in light of many social changes for women religious has been critical in not only reflecting, but also in helping them to construct social change, specifically by its role in symbolic interaction processes related to the formation and perpetuation of personal identity.

Research Method

The twenty-six women who participated in this study are members of non-cloistered orders in western Massachusetts, USA. These orders adopted secular dress in the 1960s and 1970s. Other American orders that were in the forefront of changing dress started as early as the late 1950s.[1]

One-hour, open-ended and transcribed interviews on their experience of exchanging religious habit for secular dress have allowed me to examine social and psychological implications of this event from a personal perspective rather than examining this issue as a strictly social phenomenon. Some feminist researchers propose that women interviewing other women is a particularly effective method due to common understandings in woman-to-woman talk (Reinharz, 1992).

My research follows an inductive, grounded theory approach, originally proposed by Glaser and Strauss (1967) and later examined as an effective method for textiles and clothing research by Boynton-Arthur (1993). More specifically, my interest in a symbolic interaction explanatory framework emerged from examining the data.

I interviewed each woman in her home or work environment, which I felt allowed her to open up concerning her personal experiences as they related to issues of dress and identity. This was important because until the time of Vatican II, personal expression, particularly in the area of dress, was extremely limited. The habit, indicating symbolic social control, reflected deeper issues of total devotion and obedience to the church. My research was facilitated by discussing relinquishing the habit, fifteen to twenty years after the event, allowing women to arrive at some degree of comfort with her identity and related appearance and ability to articulate these issues.

A significant aspect of this study is that research on women religious is sparse. Outsiders, like myself, have not been readily welcomed by women religious to conduct research within their organizations. I began my study by discussing the research with presidents of two orders, who were also leaders within the community of women religious. I found that their recommendation of other women religious who might be available for interviews, clearly opened many doors.

I found a one-to-one interview setting conducive to observing non-verbal communication. For example, their repeated postponement of a scheduled meeting, body language during the interview and what they chose to wear clearly had implications for interpretation. I have selected segments of interviews to illustrate conceptual or theoretical approaches to questions of identity work. To retain anonymity, statements will not be identified by name.

Emerging From the Habit: Fashion and Secular Clothing

The period following Vatican II was a period of emerging personal identity. During this time, the women in this study experienced profound conflicts surrounding dress and its complex relationship with their vow of poverty.

The essence of the vow of poverty of spirit is humility, which is facilitated by material poverty (Metz, 1968). The habit had come to be accepted as a visible symbol of humility, while fashion and cultural issues of women's appearance, such as make-up and hair style, were historically associated with worldliness and materialism, i.e. fashion. Yet, women religious found themselves visibly re-entering the secular world from the perspective of appearance. Because of their vow of poverty, there was little money for clothing. Most of their attire post-habit came from hand-me-downs, thrift shops, or sales. The following quote is from a woman religious who worked in a career in women's clothing sales for thirteen years prior to entering religious training. She expresses ambivalence about her love of clothes:

> I maintained my ability over the years [while in habit] to be a very good shopper. I would go to Steigers [Department Store] – the girls [clerks] would really get to know me. Many of them I had known throughout the years and they would know when the bargains were coming in. I became a shopper for several other people, especially in the early days [of transition from habits]. Now I struggle tremendously. I have far too many clothes. I'm good for a while but I have to keep looking. Someone else might not see me as a person that has a lot of clothes.

The habit had obscured visible markers of womanhood such as the hair and figure. In my interviews, much discussion focused on the personal discomfort and even trauma of re-emerging into secular society. Skills related to personal appearance had to be re-learned. Hair was discussed frequently as the focus of anxiety. After years of deprivation from air and light under the habit, hair loss was common. In this interview segment, a woman religious discusses her personal viewpoint on hair:

> Respondent: I saw older women buying wigs who had lost their hair because of the habit.
>
> Interviewer: Was that because of rubbing?
>
> Respondent: Yes and also because they didn't get air. Even at night they wore caps.
>
> Interviewer: Was this a permanent hair loss?
>
> Respondent: Yes, for some. But for some it was OK [it grew back]. I color my hair. It's something I do for myself. In the 1960s we began to do a lot of more personalized and psychological study of ourselves. The spiritual was always part of it. How can you separate the spiritual and emotional? It's holistic.

The habit had given women religious surprising freedom from the tyranny of appearance experienced by women in North American culture. Women religious were confronted with issues of body weight that had previously been obscured under the folds of black serge. Some women interviewed went on diets. Their awareness of style and fashion became evident. Women made personal choices about make-up, jewelry, modesty issues (length of skirt, neckline) and even hair coloring. The move to secular dress had a dramatic impact on both women religious and society in general. 'It revealed to the world in general the human being underneath the habit. But more important, it revealed the nun to herself: It was an experience in recognition' (Griffin, 1975, p. 79).

Women emerged from habit during the turbulent period of the Civil Rights Movement, the Vietnam War and the Women's Movement. Whether in habit or not, women religious are known for their involvement in social causes. Several women in the study referred to themselves as feminists, noting that historically they were role models for women who chose lives of dedication rather than marriage and family. Women religious also acknowledged their identities as single, professional women, struggling with their continuing conflicts with the patriarchal structure of the Vatican. They have been active participants in social activism and the dual labor market of the parish, where they have frequently, despite achieving higher education than priests, been denied positions of authority and participation in aspects of the liturgy.

The emergence of women religious from habits to secular fashion not only reflected gender controversy within the Church but also helped women to construct new identities as educated and professional women religious, rather than cloistered icons of the Church. Two women in my study referred to the identities of women prior to Vatican II as 'women of service' or more derogatively, 'handmaids of the Church'. In a symbolic feminist action after Vatican II that coincided with elimination of the habit, many women religious dropped the male component of their chosen names and reassumed the female. The names of male saints who possessed desirable virtues were assigned to the women by their Mother Superior before the women took their final vows.

> There was something else going on . . . we were changing our clothes and we were also changing our names. It didn't happen like Friday and Saturday, but it happened that we just kind of rebelled against having men's names – Sister Mary Peter, Sister Mary John, Sister Mary Bartholomew. Many women religious were moving out of their dress identity and they were changing their names back. All that was happening at the same time.

Discarding the habit was perceived by the women in this study as a positive step towards allowing them to work and interact as human beings while interpersonal distance lessened. In a positive sense, the Church, prior to

Vatican II, had viewed the habit as a protection against the evils of the world, yet that caused many religious to perceive themselves as isolated and inhibited from mingling with the people. The women's bodies were restrained and controlled by the Church within the confines of the habit. Women religious in this study perceived secular dress as essential in allowing them normal, daily, human interactions, which greatly enhanced their ability to provide social service within the community. They symbolically reclaimed their bodies as they discarded the habit.

> From 1983–87 I was in Kentucky in Appalachia. I could never have done down there in the habit what I did in my [secular] clothes. It would have been an absolute impossibility. My freedom would have been restricted. I was living in a county where there were only thirty Catholic families. I didn't go in as a Sister, I went in as a person named Mary.

Theoretical Issues

Symbolic interaction theory asserts 'that the self is established, maintained and altered in and through communication' (Stone, 1962, p. 216). Stone widened the perspective of symbolic interaction studies to include appearance as a dimension of communication, usually the precursor to verbal transactions. Furthermore, Stone asserted that appearance is a critical factor in the 'formulation of the conception of self' (Stone, 1962, p. 216). Appearance establishes identity by indicating to others what the individual projects as his or her 'program' (one's social roles of gender, age, occupation). In turn, these are 'reviewed' by others, thereby validating or challenging the self (Stone, 1962, p. 222).

> It [identity] is not a substitute word for 'self'. Instead, when one has identity, he is situated – that is, cast in the shape of a social object by the acknowledgment of his participation or membership in social relations. One's identity is established when others place him as a social object by assigning him the same words of identity that he appropriates for himself or announces. It is in the coincidence of placements and announcements that identity becomes a meaning of the self and often such placements and announcements are aroused by apparent symbols such as uniforms. The policeman's uniform, for example, is an announcement of his identity as policeman and validated by others' placements of him as policeman (Stone, 1962, p. 223).

Stone describes identity as being established by two processes, apposition and opposition, a bringing together and setting apart. 'To situate the person as a social object is to bring him together with other objects so situated and, at the same time to set him apart from still other objects. Identity, to Stone, is intrinsically associated with all the joinings and departures of social life. To have an identity is to join with some and depart from others, to enter and leave social relations at once' (Stone, 1962, p. 223).

In contrast to Stone, Goffman defines personal identity as 'the assumption that the individual can be differentiated from all others' (Goffman, 1963, p. 57). From an interactionist perspective, this was a real dilemma for some women religious in habit. Their dress clearly symbolized their total affiliation to their work in the order, but was described by them as 'restricting' in their ability to interact and communicate freely. The consequences of these symbolic limitations led to a paradox described by the women as causing them to 'feel less than fully human.'

Snow and Anderson (1987) in their research on identity work of the homeless, noted that while distinctions are made between identity and self concept, the difference between personal and social identity is less frequently addressed. They define social identity as the attributes 'imputed to others in an attempt to place or situate them as social objects'. In contrast, personal identity refers to 'self-designations and self-attributions brought into play or asserted during the course of interaction' (Snow and Anderson, 1987, p. 1347). This definition of social and personal identity is relevant to my study, as I am examining how dress can symbolize both components of identity.

Fred Davis (1992) addressed the concept of ambivalence and appearance more directly than other symbolic interactionists who preceded him. He argued that personal identity announcements and social identity placements might not be congruous. For example, a person might dress as a police officer for a costume party and be incorrectly identified as someone who is actually responsible for law enforcement. Davis (1992, p. 25), maintaining that dress serves as 'a kind of visual metaphor for identity . . . registering the culturally anchored ambivalence that resonates with and among identities,' suggests that personal and social identity incongruity occurs regularly because dress is often an ambivalent form of communication. Davis (1992) is broadly interested in dress and its symbolic relationship to identity, but more specifically, he discusses his theories within the framework of fashion. Davis defines fashion by distinguishing it from style, custom, conventional or acceptable dress, or prevalent modes by stressing the importance of the element of change (p. 14). While the term dress communicates elements of stability, use of the term fashion implies the added element of social change (Roach-Higgins and Eicher, 1993).

A symbolic interaction perspective emphasizes social process and meaning(s) and is relevant for explaining how and why these women negotiated their visual and verbal awareness of their appearance (Kaiser, Nagasawa and Hutton, 1995). When the women emerged as visible females from the self-described 'androgyny' of how they felt in the habit, identity conflicts surfaced.[2] Davis (1992) described how dress serves as 'a kind of visual metaphor for identity . . . registering the culturally anchored ambivalences that resonate with and among identities.' Ambivalence was acknowledged by Davis (1992, p. 25) to be natural and integral to human experience and can be exhibited in symbolic issues of appearance.

The dialectic of the women's physical body, symbolized by their dress, to the social body of the Roman Catholic church, is a critical one in understanding the power of dress in both reflecting and constructing social change for women religious. For example, Marx (1967) and Durkheim and Mauss (1963) all argued for the dialectic between the natural and social body. Other social scientists have viewed the body as the *tabula rasa* for socialization. Van Gennep (1960), Mauss (1973), Bordieu (1977) and Douglas (1966, 1970) have argued this dialectic to demonstrate the social construction of the body.

Comaroff's research (1985) on the *Tshidi* people of South Africa bears an interesting and instructive relationship to this study of women religious. Comaroff examined the manner in which symbolic 'schemes' (for example, dress) mediate structure and practice. Through both historical research and anthropological fieldwork, she analyzed how the body mediates between self and society, specifically through her analysis of uniforms worn by both men and women in the post-missionary and post-colonial Zionist church in South Africa. She discovered how these uniforms mediated a complex interdependence between domination and resistance, change and perpetuation. Likewise, she explored the meaning of liminality in such a context. Liminality is defined as an inter-structural or transitional situation during rites of passage (Van Gennep, 1960; Turner, 1967). In the case of the *Tshidi*, uniforms symbolized the transition they made from liminality, created by radical social and cultural change, to political resistance.

Comaroff explains how uniforms attained an important role in all South African churches from the start by distinctively marking converts as those who were 'civilized' by the missionary message. Whereas indigenous dress, i.e. pre-colonial appearances, clearly made visual the female and male reproductive body, the uniform of the Zionist church covered not only the organs of reproduction, but obscured visual signs of femininity, masculinity and social status. Comaroff concluded that this appearance, through many signs that were comprehended by members of that society, were acknowledged to be symbols of mediated power.

In this manner, Zionist dress, like the bricolages of such protest movements as cargo cults, appropriates select signs of colonial dominance, turning historical symbols of oppression into dynamic forces of transcendence. With the same logic, the satin banners incorporate military pomp, evoking the aggressive Protestant image of 'soldiers of the Lord'; the letter H affixed to them suggests perhaps a double cross, but is also emblematic of the power of literacy itself . . . . For literacy has been a crucial marker of the forces that subjugate the uneducated peasant (Comaroff, 1985, p. 225–26).

Comaroff's research sheds light on the case of the women religious and their different but related set of issues. The *Tshidi* used symbols of resistance, i.e. dress, related to both colonialism and the missionaries in mediating their identity. In a similar manner, the women religious in this study also used dress in their politics of resistance to emerge from their socialization into the order prior to Vatican II to the liminality surrounding Vatican II and finally the mediation of their social and personal identity. In both studies, the spirit of resistance was one that facilitated the reality of existing within the respective social systems. Like the *Tshidi* who adapted to colonialism and the missionaries, women religious in this study during a period of demanded social change chose to remain within their orders rather than abandon them. For both the *Tshidi* and the women religious, their new identities symbolically reflected and constructed by their dress demonstrated their ability to protest and yet remain within the system. Their ability to appropriate fashions of the secular world indicated their ability to mediate between the demands of a consumer society and their vow of poverty.

Conclusion

This study of women religious provides a model for examining how changes in enduring modes of dress such as habits can be examined not only in relation to the more predominantly held view of changing social roles but also from the perspective of personal identity. The relationship between dress and social change must be carefully examined, as with women religious, by examining their relationship to social role, issues of social and personal identity, and their mediation through the symbol of dress.

Davis (1992, p. 26) uses the term *fault lines* to describe 'culturally induced strains concerning who and what we are' that find expression in dress. Vatican II certainly created an enormous quake for women religious, but the forces of change within orders ultimately came from the women themselves in the form of human agency. Women religious were poised and ready to address issues of role, identity and social change.

Notes

1. This material is based upon work supported by the Cooperative State Research, Extension, Education Service, US Department of Agriculture, Massachusetts Agricultural Experiment Station, under Project No. 728.

2. Some women in the study used this word to elaborate on how they felt wearing a habit. This is not my choice of words. The term *androgyny* is derived from the Greek word *andro* (male) and *gyn* (female). Heilbrun (1964) uses this term to define a condition in which the characteristics of the sexes and the human impulses expressed by men and women are not rigidly assigned. Therefore, the term may be more closely associated with perceptions of identity than solely of characteristics associated with physical appearance.

References

Aherne, M. C. (1983). *Joyous service: The history of the Sisters of Saint Joseph of Springfield*. Holyoke: Sisters of Saint Joseph.

Bordieu, P. (1977). *Outline of a theory of practice*. Trans. R. Nice. Cambridge: Cambridge University Press.

Boynton-Arthur, L. (1993). The applicability of ethnography and grounded theory to clothing and textile research. In S. Lennon & L. Burns (eds.), *ITAA Special Publication #5* (pp. 137–45). Monument, CO: ITAA.

Comaroff, J. (1985). *Body of power, spirit of resistance*. Chicago, IL: University of Chicago Press.

Davis, F. (1992). *Fashion, culture and identity*. Chicago, IL: University of Chicago Press.

Douglas, M. (1966). *Purity and danger: An analysis of concepts of pollution and taboo*. Washington: Frederick Praeger.

Douglas, M. (1970). *Natural symbols*. New York: Vintage Books.

Durkheim, E. and Mauss, M. (1963). *Primitive classification*. Trans. R. Needham, London: Cohen & West.

Ebaugh, H. (1977). *Out of the cloister: A study of organizational dilemmas*. Austin: University of Texas Press.

Ebaugh, H. (1993). *Women in the vanishing cloister*. New Brunswick, NJ: Rutgers University Press.

Goffman, E. (1963). *Stigma: Notes on the management of a spoiled identity*. Englewood Cliffs, NJ: Prentice Hall.

Glaser, B. and Strauss, A. (1967). *The discovery of grounded theory*. Chicago: Aldine Publishing Co.

Griffin, M. (1975). Unbelling the cat. *The courage to choose*. Boston: Little Brown.

Heilbrun, C. (1964). *Toward a recognition of androgyny*. New York: Alfred A. Knopf, Inc.

Kaiser, S., Nagasawa, R. & Hutton, S. (1995). Construction of an SI theory of fashion: Part 1, ambivalence and change. *Clothing and Textiles Research Journal 13 (3),* 172–83.

Lifton, J. (1961). *Thought reform and the psychology of totalism.* New York: Norton.

Marx, K. (1967). *Capital: A Critique of Political Economy,* 3 vols. New York: International Publishers.

Metz, J. (1968). *Poverty of spirit.* NY: Paulist Press.

Mauss, M. (1973). Techniques of the Body. Trans. B. Brewster. *Economy and Society, 2 (1):* 70–88.

Reinharz, S. (1992). *Feminist methods in social research.* Oxford: Oxford University Press.

Roach-Higgins, M. & Eicher, J. (1993). Dress and identity. *ITAA Special Publication #5.*

Snow, D. & Anderson, L. (1987). Identity work among the homeless: The verbal construction and avowal of personal identities. *American Journal of Sociology, 92 (6),* 1336–71.

Stone, G. (1962). Appearance and the self. In A. Rose (ed.) *Human behavior and social processes: An interactionist approach* (pp. 86–118). New York: Houghton, Mifflin, Co.

Turner, V. (1967). *The forest of symbols.* Ithaca: Cornell University Press.

VanGennep, A. (1960). *The rites of passage.* Trans. M.B. Vizedom and G. L. Caffee. Chicago: University of Chicago Press.

9

The 'Paarda' Expression of Hejaab Among Afghan Women in a Non-Muslim Community[1]

M. Catherine Daly

The variations of Muslim women's head coverings are often seen by non-Muslims as essential markers of a woman's personal, social and cultural identity in Islamic society.[2] Head coverings and related practices are often portrayed in the print and visual media; these visual impressions have tended to depersonalize, essentialize and even objectify Muslim women as no more than a head covering. In many instances the practice of women wearing head coverings associated with Islamic affiliation is frequently maligned by *etics* or 'outsiders' as a form of female oppression, an ethnic stereotype and a kind of religious orthodoxy.[3] In contrast to this view, the goal of this chapter is to provide balance with an *emic* or 'insider's' perspective of the *paarada* expression of *hejaab* among Afghan women living in a non-Muslim community in the United States.

Based on ethnographic research in an urban community in the midwestern United States, this chapter's focus is on the Islamic practice of *hejaab*; 'to cover one's head.' Known as *paarda* in Afghan *Dari*, *hejaab* is expressed by Afghan women living in a non-Muslim community by wearing a head covering called a *chaadar*. To illuminate this practice, there are two foci in this chapter. The first objective is to describe the ethno-aesthetics and visual characteristics of the *chaadar*, worn by Afghan women in the United States.[4] The second objective is to discuss the contextual flexibility of women's head covering practices comparing and contrasting their public and private use in non-Afghan communities.[5] The summary concludes with comments about the use of the *chaadar* and its social meaning as an example of the inter-relatedness of gender and ethnic and religious identity.[6] The pertinent question is, from an Afghan woman's point of view, what does it mean to be a woman, to be Afghan and to be Muslim by virtue of wearing this distinctive item, a *chaadar*?

Socio-cultural Background

The Afghan women interviewed included those women who are the eldest in the community; those whose ages ranged from forty to seventy years old. These eight women from approximately sixty-five to seventy families living within a non-Muslim community, are considered the most respected women in the Afghan community. They are respected not only because of their generational status within the community but because of their adherence to traditional Afghan and Islamic practices, which is reflected in their practice of *paarda*.

Each woman was interviewed in her home for a minimum of two hours for three meetings. A female Afghan interpreter was used. During all interviews younger women in the family were present. The older women were also questioned informally during more public situations when they gathered together with both men and women on special occasions in the Afghan community. These events included general celebrations such as on *Nowroz*, the first day of spring; familial events such as *shaway shash*, the sixth day celebration following childbirth; *naam zaadee,* engagement ceremonies; and *nikaah,* wedding ceremonies, in addition to religious occasions such as *Ramazaan* and *Mosque* attendance.

All the women interviewed were born and married in Afghanistan. Prior to marriage many of the women lived in the more rural areas of the thirty-three Afghan provinces. As most Afghan women recall, 'Life was best there; we were free to do as we pleased.' Following their marriage most of the women moved to more urban and at times socially constrained metropolitan settings with their husbands. They lived in these more urban environments and established families prior to their departure from Afghanistan. Regardless of the locations in which they subsequently lived following marriage, when asked where they were from, all referred to their village or province of birth. Though Afghan kinship observes patrilineal and patrilocal patterns of familial relationships, Afghan women demonstrate a knowledge of their family origin and geographic location when given an opportunity.

During the '1979 Afghan Coup,' or Soviet invasion of Afghanistan, with some prior planning, each of the women interviewed had fled Afghanistan with either partial or intact extended families. As each woman replied, 'We told everyone we were going on vacation.' Interviewees traveled with their children and families or, if separate from their husbands, with an uncle or

women throughout the world. When Afghan women practice *paarda* they cover part of the body such as the head, including the hair, neck and shoulders. A more conservative interpretation of *paarda* is to cover the entire body, wearing a *chaadaree* or complete veil. The interpretation of a *chaadar* worn in a Muslim community varies depending on the culture, ethnic group, geographic region, rural and urban locations. Currently this distinction between type of head covering worn by Afghan women is an important issue among the various groups claiming Islamic sovereignty in Afghanistan. For example, the Taliban, which is a presumed fundamentalist group, strictly interprets the *Qur'an* by enforcing *paarda* and require women to wear the *chaadaree* in addition to the *chaadar* in public, regardless of age, status or religious affiliation.

To wear a *chaadar* in a non-Muslim community, such as the United States, is a more liberal practice among Afghans than it would be in Afghanistan because the *chaadar* is not customarily worn by non-Muslims. From a non-Muslim point of view, wearing a *chaadar* is considered a conservative Islamic practice because it is perceived as a religious garment worn in a secular context. The *chaadar* is acknowledged by non-Muslims as a form of religious observance and may even pass for a familiar scarf. The *chaadaree* has less precedence in use and therefore Afghans choose not to wear it in the United States because of its perceived extreme connotations.[11]

As suggested earlier, there are many style variations and personal preferences for how the *chaadar* is worn, although most are a two-dimensional square or rectangular shaped fabrics. *Chaadar* are worn by young girls as a small square scarf or *dismal* tied symmetrically under the chin, while women wear larger squares and rectangles as scarves and shawls over the head with the ends draped in a variety of positions. Others are worn as shawls draped either over the back of the neck over the shoulders to the front, or draped from front to back over the shoulders.

Draped styles are asymmetrical and depending on whether one is right- or left-handed, longer on the right or left side of the body. Typically, a *chaadar* is draped longer on the side of the handedness of the wearer, that is, if right-handed the longer edge of the *chaadar* is longer on the right-hand side. Consequently, the reverse is true if wearer is left handed with the longer edge on the left-hand side.

Ethno-Aesthetics

Typically *chaadar* are square (45′ × 45′) or rectangular (85′ × 45′), two-dimensional shaped fabrics. The size of either shape varies from 'small' to 'large.' The dimensions are dependent to a degree on the loomed width of the fabric purchased for *chaadar* or head coverings. The size of *chaadar* also coordinates with the style of clothing worn, the season of the year and the occasion. 'This one is nice, it keeps me warm. I wear it mostly during the winter.' For example, a lightweight wool challis head covering during cool weather and on more formal occasions, may be preferable in contrast to a heavier weight wool *chaadar* worn during the winter months.

Some head coverings are hand-woven, but the majority are made of commercially woven fabrics from Afghanistan, Pakistan, India and China. Most Afghan women prefer finely woven silk *chaadar* but cotton and wool are acceptable depending on season and context. As one woman stated with a smile, 'Silk is my favorite.' Silk is preferred not only because of the luxuriousness of the fiber and the prestige of wearing silk, but primarily because of its drape, hand and texture. Most silk *chaadar* are solid white but those that have surface designs are either tone-on-tone machine or hand embroidered with small geometric or floral patterns.

From an Afghan woman's point of view, the hand or feel of the fabric is the most important characteristic of any *chaadar*. As one Afghan woman suggested, 'I can close my eyes and feel by the touch of my hand.' Generally acceptable fabrics for *chaadar* include finely woven silk crepe, which provides texture due to the structure of the crepe weave. Since living in the United States, few Afghan women purchase *chaadar* fabric locally. Several Afghan women mentioned that 'The fabric is inferior. It doesn't feel right or good.' Texture is an important characteristic because it contributes to the proper drape, another characteristic that is valued. Crepe *chaadar* 'appear' soft as well as 'feel soft,' which is visible as it will flow with subtle bodily movements.

Chaadar may be purchased with edges unfinished, or finished with machine-stitching, or hand-worked hems that are either rolled, beaded or fringed. A more recent occurrence is the introduction of commercially produced lace trims and hand crocheted edges. One woman favored these because 'my friend crocheted the edges.' These more innovative techniques are personal touches when *chaadar* are given as gifts; they are then treasured because of these relationships.

The favored color choice of *chaadar* is white, *safayd*, because it is associated with the requisite white head covering worn during the *Hajj* or pilgrimage to Mecca which all Muslims are required to make once in their lifetime. White is then subsequently worn after making one's pilgrimage, or by those who aspire to make a pilgrimage, or by those acknowledging their religiosity. Also when husbands or male relatives return from their *Hajj* they may return with many *chaadar* as gifts. White *chaadar* are also worn weekly on Friday, *Juma*, the holy day when Muslims attend Mosque.

In addition to the color white, older women tend to wear muted and darker *chaadar* that are also made of heavier fabrics. Heavier, darker and black *(ceyar)*, colored head coverings are also worn during cooler months. Some are made of wool, may even be plaid and are worn for special occasions. In contrast, younger women wear more lively, highly saturated colors frequently in floral patterns and gold metallic embroideries. It is also common to see young women wear vibrant green *(sabz)*, *chaadar* embroidered in gold metallic embroidery for festive occasions when velvet dresses *(kaalaayi afghanee)* and satin pants *(tumbaan)* are worn.

Surface designs on both hand-woven and commercial woven textiles include regionalized styles, patterns and techniques of embroidery. Sewing and embroidery are acceptable sustainable textile arts for Afghan women in Afghanistan. Some styles are more figurative and floral, while others more geometric. Dupaigne (1993) documented embroidered items of apparel including hats, dresses and bags of Afghanistan's nomadic peoples. But little is known of either regional urban or rural Afghan embroidery traditions and especially of embroideries of Afghan women's *chaadar* or *chaadaree* outside of Afghanistan. Regional embroidery styles most frequently mentioned because of their aesthetic value include those from Kandahar and Herat (Doubleday, 1988); 'These are exquisite.'

Preferred Characteristics and Their Contextual Flexibility

In many instances the preferred physical and visual characteristics of *chaadar* are directly related to the social contexts in which they are worn. These social contexts may be interpreted in a number of ways but over-simplify personal, social and cultural interpretations. For this reason *chaadar* are a multi-vocal symbol in part situationally defined by the context in which they are worn and the individuals present.

The wearing of a *chaadar* varies according to the private versus public context in which they are worn. Events in the Afghan community are either religious or secular, casual or formal and are attended by Afghans only, or both Afghans and non-Afghans. As stated earlier, the practice of *paarda* and the liberal versus conservative manner in which a *chaadar* is worn reinforces the significance of the situation. The smaller, square *chaadar* secured under the chin is less formal, worn in private by young girls while a larger *chaadar* worn by women and draped, suggests a more formal situation.

For daily wear *chaadar* are more casual as they be worn continuously throughout the day both in the private context of the home or when 'doing' errands in a more public context in a non-Afghan community. The chaadar for everyday wear may be made of less costly materials. Those worn at home may be favorite cotton or silk ones that are threadbare with continued use. They are worn for comfort, ease of movement and performance while moving from one activity to the next. Several women referred to a favored *chaadar*, worn while praying at home. The soft creped texture contrasts with the smooth texture of Afghan women's hair. It 'sticks' or adheres to the hair, demanding less manipulation and interference with household and childcare activities.

In contrast to daily wear, *chaadar* worn for special occasions may meet additional criteria of the social function in which they are worn. *Chaadar* worn in these contexts may or may not be comfortable and may or may not provide as much freedom of movement. Metallic brocade *chaadar* fit these characteristics. Depending on the age of the wearer the *chaadar* may have other functional qualities such as those of draped silk chiffon fabrics used by young adult women while dancing.

Issues of Gender, Ethnic and Religious Identity

The *hejaab* practice of Islam has been a focal point for the dominant discourse of Muslim women's rights and sustainability in those societies that are predominately governed by religious authority. It is a complex rhetoric of perceptions about Muslim women, Islam and the head covering practices associated with *hejaab*.[12] Whether living in Afghanistan or the Afghan diaspora, Afghan women's dress including the *chaadar* and *chaadaree* visually communicates the wearer's affinity to *hejaab* or *paarda*.

Visual distinctions extend to the partial veil or *chaadar* as a marker of generational and gender status. Traditionally in Afghan culture once a young girl entered puberty and started menstruating she wore a *chaadar* as a marker of her change to adult female status and marriageability (Dupree, 1978, p. 212). In the United States, as a young girl matures she will wear *chaadar* more frequently during special events among Afghans in non-Muslim communities; its use is not so literally interpreted.

Dupree (1978) also notes that the *chaadar* is also a marker of the socio-economic status of a woman and her family, especially in those circumstances when the *chaadar* is made of expensive materials that are not accessible to others. Women take great pride in selecting *chaadar* that are in good condition and repair when worn in public for Afghan events. And as they become worn with use they are then relegated to a more private context of the home.

To wear a *chaadar* on a daily basis is not necessarily a biological or social imperative for Afghans living in non-Muslim communities. It is a matter of personal choice with varying degrees of social conformity related to more than religious observance. But it is a more customary practice for adolescent and adult women to wear *chaadar* during the periodic occasions of Afghan celebratory occasions in these communities. During these occasions, the wearing of *chaadar* provides recognition to Afghan values of both generational and gender status; a special occasion is an opportunity for elder Afghan women to continue to wear their *chaadar* while for younger Afghan women it is an opportunity to 'practice' wearing them.

Younger women generally wear more brightly colored *chaadar* with additional surface designs, while older women wear less colorful *chaadar* with less embellishments. Costliness of materials for *chaadar* are a possible indicator of the age of the wearer. For example, younger women may wear costly but machine-embroidered ones, while older women wear costly hand-embroidered *chaadar*. Younger women may wear more commercial rather than hand-manufactured *chaadar*, and older women may wear *chaadar* perceived as culturally costly heirlooms treasured because of their age. However, if a family has the financial resources, they purchase costly ones for the younger women.

Dupree (1978) notes that 'in Afghan culture women symbolize the honor of the family, the tribe and the nation, a belief which traditionally has meant that ideal female behavior was passive, modest and obedient.' Afghan women respond to this stereotype, 'we do these things out of love and respect for our husband and our family,' as opposed to Dupree's characterization. 'We are not oppressed as Americans would believe.' To wear a *chaadar* is recognized as ideal female behavior among older Afghan men and women living in non-Afghan communities.[13] Wearing a *chaadar* is more than ideal female behavior; it is an acknowledgement of the general support for the attitudes, values and beliefs of Islam and Afghan culture. To wear a *chaadar* provides a visible symbol of religiosity and cultural embeddedness that strongly communicates this message.

To an outsider or non-Muslim the wearing of a veil or *chadaar* is more strongly associated with a religious connotation of Islamic affiliation than either gender or ethnic identity. But for those who are Muslim, regional and ethnic differences distinguish the wearer. Fawzi El-Solh and Mabro (1994, p. 1) reiterate this point; 'not all Muslim women feel compelled to resort to dress or other symbolism to signal their adherence to Islam and to the Muslim component of their identity.'

As Olesen (1994, p. 44) points out, 'A striking feature of Afghanistan is its ethnic multiplicity, with its many languages and local dialects.' The largest ethnic group are the Pashtuns, followed by Tajiks, Uzbecks and Hazaras. Language coupled with religion provides major boundaries for the cultural identity of different ethnic groups (Christensen, 1995). This sense of ethnic multiplicity is acknowledged by Afghans in non-Muslims communities in the United States. Differentiation is made among Afghans when speaking, addressing and referring to a particular family who speak a language as well as come from a region that differs from their own.

A sense of ethnic multiplicity is also suggested in the wearing of a *chaadar.* In Afghanistan, the wearing of a *chaadar* is dictated by local custom and regionalism (Tapper, 1977, p. 163) which has led to stereotypes regarding the head covering practices of women. The stereotypes refer to differences between rural and uncovered, urban and covered and nomadic free-spirited women.[14] To a degree these stereotypes suggest the economic status and mobility of the various ethnic groups that are regionally defined.[15] However for Afghans living outside of Afghanistan, the wearing of *chaadar* in a non-Muslim community indicates the personal expression of ethnic pride equivalent to a national identity and affiliation.

In contrast to Afghanistan and in non-Muslim communities in the US, life in many refugee camps is controlled by resistance parties that vary from liberal to conservative observance of Islam. Regardless of orientation, all support the institution of *paarda* and believe women's place is in the home (Christensen, 1995, p. 26). In part this support may be due to the competition for scarce resources and the variability of the ethnic origins of neighbors living in close proximity with one another.

The imposition of the *chaadaree* then serves to protect Afghan women in unstable environments. The current political environment in the refugee camps and Afghanistan is dominated by the *Taliban;* a conservative Islamic group that strictly interprets Islamic practices, including *paarda.* Their edicts in the past few years govern 'the proper Islamic appearance of women in public' which includes wearing the complete body veil, *chaardaree* (Rashid, 1992, p. 29). For those women who defy these rules there are dire consequences for both women and their families.

Mayotte (1992, p. 155) writes of the personal honor of Afghan men and women that extends from gender and family to the conceptualization of the region and nation. To non-Afghans this sense of honor and protection may seem outdated and provincial in the non-Muslim communities in which Afghans live. But the Afghan's strong sense of national and ethnic identity derives from Afghanistan's strategic location in Central Asia and the enduring centuries of invasions through its boundaries (Hopkirk, 1994).

Honor, loyalty and pride are reflected through Afghan material culture that decorates home interiors and the *paarda* expression of wearing the *chaadar* in non-Muslim communities. Though few Afghans in the study referred to the concept of *paarda* defining the domestic environment, all but one woman worked outside the home with the acknowledged belief that their primary contribution was to the domestic environment.

As in the refugee camps, what potentially unites Afghans beyond gender and ethnic differences in non-Muslim communities is Islam.[16] This is evident during Mosque attendance where Muslims of all nationalities attend Friday prayer. In this context a head covering is required of all Muslim women regardless of their ethnicity or country of origin. During festive occasions, especially those of a religious nature, Afghans invite non-Afghan Muslims to attend. With such diversity in Muslim head covering practices, the result is that there is a greater variation in the numbers of women who wear head coverings, as well as the head covering styles.

Conclusion and Implications

In summary, the focus of this chapter was to describe and explore the social meaning of *chaadar* and *chaadaree* and the process of wearing these head coverings by Afghan women living in a heterogeneous American community. This exploration was accomplished by defining and describing the ethno-aesthetics and the visual characteristics of both head coverings, with particular emphasis on the more frequently worn *chaadar*; determining the contextual flexibility of *chaadar* practices; and analyzing the social use of *chaadar* as they relate to issues of identity. The reasons for wearing a *chaadar* are numerous, but what is evident is that Afghan women in the United States are responding to a 'new' historical and cultural context from that of Islamic Afghanistan that challenges their gendered, ethno-religious identity and the *paarda* expression of *chaadar* (Brenner, 1996, p. 690).

The implications of studying Afghan women's head covering practices are of value in several significant ways. The *chaadar* and *chaadaree* differentiate Afghan women by gender, ethnicity and religious affiliation from not only other Muslim women and ethnic groups in Central Asia, but external to the region among Muslim and non-Muslims alike. With respect to research, this is an important distinction then for scholars studying subtle distinctions in the similarities and differences in the variations in the form, the process of wearing, and the meaning of dress. But more importantly the research results are of social value for the cultures visually impacted by contrasting appearances in their communities. After all, from an Afghan woman's point of view, 'We just want to be able to practice our religion', and wearing a chaadar signifies this choice.

Notes

1. The transliteration of all Afghan Dari terms follows Burhan and Gouttierre's *Dari for Foreigners*.

2. See Brenner's 'Reconstructing self and society: Javanese Muslim women and the veil' for a similar discussion among Javanese Muslim women.

3. Ahmed infers that with respect to the Middle East Western feminist women are responsible for disproportionately inscribing Muslim women's head coverings with meaning (1992, p. 196–7).

4. Numerous examples exist which critique the Islamic practice of 'veiling' or covering the head, but few examples provide an adequate description of 'veils' or head coverings as actual items or material objects.

5. Contrary to non-Muslim perceptions of head coverings and their use, many style variations and multiple contexts determine the kind and manner worn.

6. Rarely does one social category exist singularly in relation to others, and such is the case with understanding the meaning of head coverings and the process of wearing them for Afghan women.

7. The term *chaadar* will be used for both singular and plural forms.

8. Brooks (1995) in *Nine Parts of Desire* describes various accounts of head covering practices throughout the Islamic world.

9. The Arabic term for *chaadaree* is *burqa*.

10. See Mernissi (1987, pp. 85–101) for a more detailed analysis of *hejaab* in the *Qur'an*; verse 53 of *sura* 33.

11. Gauhari (1996, pp. 14–15) shares an account of her experiences as a young woman wearing a *chaadaree*; 'To an outsider, a veil looked like a veil, nothing important to it. But to those of us who wore it there were big differences. Some veils were chic and stylish, with special shorter cap design. Veils also differed in the fineness of the eye mesh, the quality of the material and the way the numerous pleats were set, narrow pleats being considered more stylish than wide ones.'

12. For a more thorough analysis of Islamic history and hejaab practice see Mernissi's (1996) *Women's Rebellion and Islamic Memory.*

13. On one interview occasion my interpreter, a young Afghan woman who normally did not wear a *chaadar* tried one on. Her mother, nearly in tears, responded, 'Ah, you look so beautiful. I wish you would wear one more frequently.'

14. These differences, as Tapper notes, are oversimplified but contribute to the economic and ethnic stereotypes of Pashtun nomads.

15. Pedersen (1994) provides visual documentation of Afghan women's nomadic appearance including visuals of veils worn.

16. Islam is practiced by 99 percent of Afghans in Afghanistan (Christensen, 1995, p. 45).

References

Ahmed, L. (1992). *Women and gender in Islam: Historical roots of a modern debate.* New Haven: Yale University Press.

Brenner, S. (1996). Reconstructing self and society: Javanese Muslim women and 'the veil'. *American Ethnologist.* 690.

Brooks, G. (1995). *Nine parts of desire: The hidden world of Islamic women.* New York, NY: Anchor Books Doubleday.

Burhan, M., and Goutierre, T. (1983). *Dari for foreigners.* Omaha: Center for Afghanistan Studies.

Christensen, A. (1995). *Aiding Afghanistan: The background and prospects for reconstruction in a fragmented society.* Copenhagen: Nordic Institute of Asian Studies.

Doubleday, V. (1988). *Three women of Herat.* London: Jonathan Cape.

Dupaigne, B. (1993). *Afghan embroidery.* Lahore, Pakistan: Ferozsons Ltd.

Dupree, L. (1980). *Afghanistan.* Princeton: Princeton University Press.

Dupree, N. (1978). Behind the veil in Afghanistan. *Asia, 1 (2),* 10–15.

Fawzi El-Solh, C. and Mabro, J. (1995). *Muslim women's choices: Religious belief and social reality.* Providence: Berg Publishers.

Gauhari, F. (1996). *Searching for Saleem: An Afghan woman's odyssey.* Lincoln: University of Nebraska Press.

Hopkirk, P. (1994). *The great game: The struggle for empire in Central Asia.* New York: Kodansha International.

Mayotte, J. (1992). *Disposable people? The plight of refugees.* Maryknoll: Orbis Books.

Mernissi, F (1987). *Beyond the veil: Male-female dynamic in modern Muslim society.* Bloomington: Indiana University Press.

Mernissi, F (1996). *Women's rebellion and Islamic memory.* New York: Zed Books.

Miller, N. (1978). *Faces of change, five rural societies in transition: Bolivia, Kenya, Afghanistan, Taiwan, China Coast.* Lebanon: Wheelock Education Resources.

Olesen, A. (1994). *Afghan craftsmen: The cultures of three itinerant communities.* New York: Thames and Hudson.

Pedersen, G. (1994). *Afghan nomads in transition: A century of change among the Zala Khan Khel.* New York: Thames and Hudson.

Rashid, A. (1992). Behind the veil, again: Kabul's women don chadors and wonder about Islamic rule. *Far Eastern Economic Review,* 28–9.

Scarce, J. (1974). The development of women's veils in Persia and Afghanistan. *Costume, 8,* 4–13.

Tapper, N. (1977). Pastun nomad women in Afghanistan. *Asian Affairs, 8 (2).*

10

Hasidic Women's Head Coverings: A Feminized System of Hasidic Distinction

Barbara Goldman Carrel

Terence Turner, in his article on the Kayapo social body (1995), asserts that in all human cultures, 'collectively standardized modifications of the body surface' serve not only as embodied representations of social identity but also as basic techniques for the (re)production of social relations (pp. 146–7). In this vein, I will examine the quintessential symbol of Hasidic womanhood, her head covering, as the embodied representation of a feminized Hasidic identity as well as an embodied symbol which classifies the women of the Hasidic communities of Brooklyn, New York in terms of religiosity.[1]

The ethnographic literature which serves to explore Hasidic clothing as a symbolic articulation of a distinctive Hasidic identity and culturally meaningful principles has done so overwhelmingly from the Hasidic male perspective (Poll, 1962; Yoder, 1969, 1972). Most renowned is Solomon Poll's demonstration, in his 1962 ethnography of the Satmar Hasidim, that distinctions in Hasidic men's dress symbolically correspond to the categories and relations constitutive of the social hierarchy of the Satmar community. He states that with regard to the masculine mode of Hasidic dress:

> The types of Hasidic [men's] clothing and the [masculine] ways of looking Hasidic change from class to class. The extent of affiliation with Hasidism determines the particular kinds of garment worn. The different types of Hasidic garments serve as identifying symbols of social rank (1962, p. 65).

In this chapter, I will demonstrate that although Hasidic women dress in contemporary 'western fashions,' the female Hasidic body does display 'collectively standardized modifications.' The head covering represents one such culturally significant modification. I will begin with a brief account of

Hasidism along with the religious, cultural and historical foundations of Hasidic women's head coverings in order to situate these women within the larger community of Jewish women. A ranked order of Hasidic women's head coverings, mirroring Poll's (1962) delineation of the Satmar Hasidim's social stratification based on Hasidic men's dress, will follow. I will then elaborate on the dynamics involved in the production, maintenance and legitimation of Hasidic women's social hierarchy drawing on Pierre Bourdieu's theory of distinction (1984). Finally, I will examine the symbolic significance of hair and its control in relation to the hierarchy provided.

Hasidism as a Way of Life

Hasidism is more than religious doctrine. The movement which began in eighteenth-century Eastern Europe constitutes a way of life, serving as the basis for the culturally distinct (yet pluralistic) Hasidic world view, lifestyle and religious identity. Hasidism parallels traditional Orthodox Judaism in its strict adherence to the laws of the Torah.[2] Both Hasidism and Orthodox Jewry accept the divine revelation of the Torah which regulates not only religious observance but also the entirety of the behavior of its adherents. Despite this essential unity, as Jerome Mintz states, in *Legends of the Hasidim*:

> There are distinctions to be made between hasidim [sic] and other orthodox [sic] Jews in terms of particular traditions, customs, intensity and emphases in belief, varieties of rabbinic allegiance and social structure and organization (1968, p. 25).

First, Hasidism is characterized in terms of *ultraorthodoxy*. The word *hasidim*, which translates as 'pious ones,' connotes the Hasidic passion for the intensely fervent and extra fulfillment of Jewish law. In this sense, Hasidic prayer, ritual and conduct may be viewed as being shaped by the hyperbolization of religious precepts in an attempt to construct protective fences around those precepts to guarantee safe distance from either consciously or unconsciously transgressing Jewish law (B. Kirshenblatt-Gimblett, personal communication, 1992).

Second and perhaps the most characteristic sociological feature distinguishing the Hasidim, is the role of the *rebbe* (master) who serves as the paramount authority in the community. Believed to possess a higher soul, he is exalted as a spiritual intermediary between God and man. Discrete Hasidic communities, named after the European towns in which their group originated, are anchored to individual *rebbes*. Each Hasidic community, directed by its *rebbe*, accentuates and exemplifies particular elements of Hasidic spiritual

nature of social relations embodied in this hierarchy and (d) the ideological construct which serves to legitimize (and ultimately reproduce) this social order.

Bourdieu's Theory of Cultural Distinction

In *Distinction*, Bourdieu declares that social position is embodied in and displayed through class-based modes of culture acquisition. That is, individuals, guided by the mediating cultural lens of a class 'habitus' (lifestyle), make culturally constituted choices which produce and display different and ranked forms of cultural distinction. These choices, revealed in distinct modes of consuming and appropriating consumer goods and cultural practices, embody, display and assert an individual's position within the social order (1984).

Social relations are thus objectified in the consumption of even the most familiar objects, often 'most marked in the ordinary choices of everyday existence, such as furniture, clothing or cooking' (1984, p. 77). These class-based modes of consumption and appropriation, both the products and producers of social identity and status positions, advance the spiritual reproduction of the system. Distinct class-based symbolic forms are associated with different and ranked levels of cultural competence. Cultural competence is based on the amount and distribution of two forms of capital: (a) economic capital, or power exercised through material accumulation and economic control and (b) cultural capital, or (symbolic) power exercised through non-material accumulation and control such as education or social origin (Bourdieu, 1984). In Bourdieu's system of social distinction, the aesthetic disposition and symbolic forms of the dominant class are deemed the most valuable. All other class aesthetics and modes of consumption and appropriation are established and assigned differential value in negative dialectic relation to the dominant aesthetic.

Hasidic Men's Dress Distinctions

Poll (1962 p. 67) delineates six distinct and hierarchically ordered manifestations of Hasidic men's dress based on the presence or absence of some distinguishing features of the Hasidic man's dress code. Salient items include *shich* and *zocken* (slipper-like shoes and white knee socks), *shtreimel* and *bekecher* (fur hat and long silk coat), *kapote* (overcoat), *biber* hat (large-brimmed hat) and *bord und payes* (beard and side-locks).

Poll essentially explains Satmar social stratification in terms of cultural capital, or the frequency and intensity of religious observance and economic capital, or standing in the community based on occupation, income and material accumulation – categories central to Bourdieu's analysis as well. Because of the fundamental religious constitution of this particular community, Poll declares that Hasidic stratification is 'based primarily upon frequency and intensity of religious observance' (1962, p. 59) and maintains that:

> The criteria by which the Hasidic community is stratified are not the same as in other American communities. Lineage, wealth, occupation, income, residence, morals and manners and education operate differently. Such criteria do not determine status *unless they are associated with ritualistic observance . . . [italics added]* (1962, p. 60–1).

Thus, cultural capital (status) prevails over economic capital (economic class position) in structuring the Satmar symbolic system of distinction and determining the relations between and positioning of, the hierarchically ordered categories within the Hasidic community.

With reference to the social hierarchy of the Satmar community, Poll states that *with or without wealth*, the *rebbes* are the top-ranking religious leaders. He then defines the legitimate male Hasidic aesthetic expression and mode of cultural appropriation as being symbolically embodied in the *rebbes'* clothing, which consists of the most highly valorized signs of the Hasidic men's dress code:

> The *rebbes* are the only ones who, as a class and without exception, wear the *shich* and *zocken*. They also wear the symbolic *shtreimel* and *bekecher*, *biber* hat and *kapote* and *bord und payes* (1962, p. 68).

All other embodied forms of aesthetic distinction are ranked in relation to the dominant aesthetic (the totality of distinctively Hasidic clothing elements) depending on the presence or absence of elements found in the *rebbe's* mode of dress.

Poll asserts that in the symbolic system of distinctions inherent in and displayed through Hasidic men's dress, social position and clothing must match. His ethnographic data reveals that 'a person who wears *zehr Hasidish* [extremely Hasidic] clothing would be ridiculed if his behavior were not consistent with his appearance' (1962, p. 66). Moreover,

> Gaining recognition in a higher social stratum is a gradual process effected by increasingly religious behavior. Individuals who display more intense religious observance are asked by the community or by the *rebbe* to put on more elaborate Hasidic garments to indicate their acceptance into a higher class (1962, p. 66).

The classifying system of distinctions embodied in the different manifestations of Hasidic men's dress thus symbolically corresponds to, legitimizes and reproduces the Satmar social hierarchy.

It is important to state clearly at this time that what I will be discussing is strictly the structure, dynamics and distinctive symbolic forms associated with Hasidic women's social order and status, not economic or occupational class categories. Further ethnographic investigation and demographic data would be necessary to empirically correlate the female social hierarchy with the Hasidic objective hierarchy as is done in Poll's investigation. Although Bourdieu maintains that any society's social hierarchy of consumers is ultimately determined by its existing economic structure, I agree with Poll that such an orientation is not suitable for the Hasidic case. This does not discount the usefulness of Bourdieu's overall theoretical framework for interpreting this ethnographic data.

Hasidic Women's Head Coverings: A Symbolic System of Distinction

Based on my ethnographic fieldwork, the typology that follows is the delineation of a feminine system of Hasidic symbolic distinctions defined in terms of and signified through the different forms of head coverings commonly worn by Hasidic women. This hierarchical system symbolically reflects, legitimizes and reproduces the structuring of female categories both within and between specific Hasidic communities. The symbolic system of distinctions based on Hasidic women's head coverings from the most religious to the least is as follows:

(1)   Women who wear a *tikhl* (scarf) only. These women wear padding under the *tikhl* to feign the appearance of height that is thought to make the woman look more attractive. *The hair is completely covered.*

(1a) Women who wear a *tikhl* but add a *schpitzel* (a piece of brown pleated material worn as a front piece under the scarf) to feign the appearance of synthetic hair.

(1b) Women who wear a *tikhl* but add a *schpitzel* made of a piece of wig that is 100 percent synthetic.

(2)   Women who wear a *sheytl* (wig) made of 100 percent synthetic hair and a *tikhl* all of the time.

(2a) Women who wear a *sheytl* made of 100 percent synthetic hair and a hat all of the time.

(2b) Women who wear a *sheytl* made of 50 percent synthetic–50 percent natural hair and a *tikhl* all of the time.

(2c) Women who wear a *sheytl* made of 50 percent synthetic–50 percent natural hair and a hat all of the time.

(2d) Women who wear a *sheytl* made of 100 percent human hair and a *tikhl* all of the time.

(2e) Women who wear a *sheytl* made of 100 percent human hair and a hat all of the time.

(3) Women who wear only a *sheytl* made of 100 percent synthetic hair.

(3a) Women who wear only a *sheytl* made of 50 percent synthetic–50 percent human hair.

(3b) Women who wear only a *sheytl* made of 100 percent human hair.

A symbolic classification of Hasidic women's dress could also include other features of clothing such as leg-coverings or length of skirt. However, head coverings offer the clearest ranking of any aesthetic feature of the Hasidic woman's dress code. Moreover, the head covering, long considered the quintessential symbol of Hasidic womanhood, most conspicuously distinguishes her from the larger New York City population of women.

This hierarchy may in fact be viewed as descending from the aesthetic expression which most uniquely distinguishes the Hasidic woman – the *tikhl* with no hair showing whatsoever – to the aesthetic expression most similar to other (non-Jewish) women in New York City – the *sheytl* made entirely of human hair. There is a religious justification for a Hasidic woman attempting to embody an aesthetic which sets her apart from the non-Jewish or non-religious Jewish woman. In addition to the Torah prescriptions determining which parts of a woman's body must be covered, there are specific *halakhoth* which identify the types clothing considered immodest and proscribed for an observant Jewish woman (Fuchs 1985, pp. 101–4). One *halakhah* states that it is a serious transgression for an observant Jewish woman, through clothing or appearance, to follow the ways of the non-Jew or non-observant Jew. 'If clothing oversteps propriety in even the smallest detail, it is a violation of the Torah injunction, 'You shall not walk in their statuses' (Fuchs, 1985, p. 101).

The symbolic system of hierarchically ordered head coverings represents Hasidic women both within and across the boundaries of different Hasidic sects in Brooklyn. Each manifestation mentioned may be found within the bounds of every sect. However, a particular preponderance of one category as opposed to another may be associated with different Hasidic communities.

For example, category (1) women, who wear a *tikhl* only, are generally associated with the women of the Satmar Hasidic community of Williamsburg, a group with the reputation of most strictly adhering to the customary ways of Eastern European Hasidism. Although the women of the Bobover Hasidic community in Borough Park can be seen wearing each mode of head covering from category (1) through category (3), many women with whom I spoke related that most women in their community do not wear a *tikhl* only. Although many women claimed to greatly admire those women who wear a *tikhl* only, they also admitted that they hadn't yet arrived at that level of religiosity. They claimed to feel more comfortable with their appearance if wearing a wig.

In Bourdieu's terms, this particular presentation of a gendered system of symbolic distinction represents the different levels of appropriating the religious principle of *tzniuth*, in particular and Hasidic religiosity and piety in general. As in Poll's delineation, distinct modes of cultural appropriation, embodied in the different manifestations of head coverings, are hierarchically ordered in terms of Hasidic cultural competence. That is, from the Hasidic perspective, the degree of Hasidic religiosity as measured by the extent to which Torah prescriptions in relation to *tzniuth* head coverings are adhered to and hyperbolized in particularly Hasidic fashion.

As indicated by Poll's ethnography (1962), the Hasidic social structure is hierarchically ordered primarily on the basis of 'cultural capital' or Hasidic religiosity rather than 'economic capital' or material accumulation. The following section from *Rebbetzin* Rubinitz's (a London *rebbetzin*, or wife of a Hasidic *rebbe*) [unpublished] lecture for women corroborates Poll's (1962) assertion that the more valorized 'capital' content in Hasidic 'cultural competence' is Hasidic religiosity or spirituality.[7] In her lecture, the *Rebbetzin* discusses the importance of leading a spiritual life, reflective of 'the world to come,' rather than being ruled by materialistic desires:

> It's not just a matter of whether you have the means or not. It's not the means that we're talking about. It's a *mide aze* of *oysakones oylem haze iker* [a mental pre-occupation with the materialistic things of this world]. And it doesn't matter whether you have the means or you don't have the means. If you have a *mide* [frame of mind] of simplicity, it's a *mide tovah* [good frame of mind]. And if you have a *mide* of being *meshuge oylem hazeh* [frame of mind of being crazy about this world] ... And this accessory and that accessory. And this thing and that thing. It's a *mide hazeh* [materialistic frame of mind].

> A love for *oylem haze* [this world] and *oylem habe* [the world to come] cannot coexist .... Like fire and water in one *keyle* [vessel], whichever one is stronger, it's going to overpower the other one. If the fire is stronger, it's going to make the water evaporate. And if the water is stronger, it's going to make the fire go out ... You can't have a life dedicated to *rukhnies* [spirituality] and want the *gashmeis*

[material things] as well . . . it can't coexist. For these people that want both, it's the greatest contradiction.

Hasidic ideology asserts that one's spiritual level of piety is genetically inherited through family lineage. The following metaphor, offered by one of the Bobover *rebbe*'s granddaughters, reveals how the legitimizing religious ideology facilitates the maintenance and reproduction of the female system of symbolic distinction and its corresponding social hierarchy.

The Bobover *rebbe*'s granddaughter discussed dress distinctions in terms of a metaphorical Hasidic ladder whereby each step of the ladder represents a different and hierarchically ordered level of religiosity and feminine modesty. Since 'everyone is born at a certain level,' each Hasidic woman must strive, from the relative and hereditary position of her own spiritual endowment, to reach a more *tzniuth* level by combating her materialistic fashion desires. She stressed that it is very important for each woman to remain cognizant of her ranked position on the ladder, for if one attempts to reach too high by 'jumping too many rungs at a time,' the consequences could be fatal. A safe climb is one rung at a time.

Suri, a Hasidic women who works in a women's clothing store in Borough Park, offers an example of how this ideology aids in reproducing the system of distinctions and the social order it reflects. In one of our conversations, she advised that a married woman should always follow the aesthetic repres-entation and level of religiosity of her husband's family by selecting the same mode of head covering as her mother-in-law. Suri also reported that Hasidic women tend to marry a man whose mother is on the same religious level and embodies a similar religious aesthetic as her own mother. Not unexpect-edly, she declared that if possible, it was always fortunate to 'marry up, but one should never marry down.'

Finally, the different and ranked modes of Hasidic women's head coverings express, assert, or defend a woman's social position or level of cultural competence. As Bourdieu asserts,

> Objectively and subjectively aesthetic stances adopted in matters like cosmetics, clothing or home decoration are opportunities to experience or assert one's position in social space, as a rank to be upheld or a distance to be kept (1984, p. 57).

Once again, Suri provides an illustration of how a woman may symbolically assert her position by selecting a certain form of head covering through the following anecdote. She divulged that customarily she wears a *sheytl* that is 50 percent synthetic/50 percent human hair (category 3a) as does her own mother. However, when she visits her husband's family, in order to please her mother-in-law, she 'upgrades' her head covering by adding a *tikhl* (category 2b).[8] Her mother-in-law, she related, is 'more religious' than she. Therefore, in order to present herself in the best possible light to her *mishpokhe* (in-laws), without having to buy an entirely different wig, she alters her appearance by adding a scarf, thus positioning herself at a comparable level to that of her mother-in-law. She explains 'Why offer a rose with the thorns showing?'

Hasidic Women's Head Coverings: A Form of Social Control

The system of social distinction displayed through the head coverings of Hasidic women may also be viewed in terms of the different and ranked levels of Hasidic socialization. Following Terence Turner, in *The Social Skin*, the head covering may be viewed as one sign in the embodied language of the Hasidic dress code through which the drama of socialization is expressed:

> The surface of the body, as the common frontier of society, the social self and the psycho-biological individual, becomes the symbolic stage upon which the drama of socialisation [sic] is enacted and bodily adornment (in all its culturally multifarious forms, from body-painting to clothing and from feather head-dresses to cosmetics) becomes the language through which it is expressed (1980, p. 112).

According to Turner, hair, in particular, represents the psycho-biological forces which must be channeled into acceptable social form:

> Hair, like skin, is a natural part of the surface of the body, but unlike skin it continually grows outward, erupting from the body into the social space beyond it. Inside the body, beneath the skin, it is alive and growing; outside, beyond the skin, it is dead and without sensation, although its growth manifests the unsocialized biological forces within. The hair on the head thus focuses the dynamic and unstable quality of the frontier between the 'natural', bio-libidinous forces of the inner body and the external sphere of social relations. In this context, hair offers itself as a symbol of the libidinal energies of the self and the never-ending struggle to constrain within acceptable forms their eruption into social space (1980, p. 116).

Ella, an Orthodox Jewish woman living in the Borough Park vicinity, explains the belief that hair is perceived as an arousing biological presence:

> The whole idea is that technically, the hair of a woman is a very sensual part of a woman. No matter how ugly the hair is. It could be the frizziest, ugliest hair. Really bad. Straggly. But it's her hair, coming out of her head. And it's nature.

Hair is, to use Turner's words, a 'symbol of the libidinal energies of the self.' The *Encyclopaedia Judaica* confirms this perception of hair, especially for married women. 'Some rabbis compared the exposure of a married woman's hair to the exposure of her privy parts' (1972, p. 6).

In discussing wigs, Suri stressed that the wig of a Hasidic woman 'should look like a wig.' It is important that the hair of her wig not be mistaken for her own hair, growing out of her head. Fuchs' delineation of the *Dath Yehudith* on appropriate head coverings for the religious woman echoes this objective. He states,

> There are authorities who prohibit wigs made from the wearer's own hair, but permit all other wigs. Some authorities forbid the use of wigs altogether, on the grounds that they often are mistaken for natural hair (Fuchs, 1985, p. 89–90).

Viewing the symbolic hierarchy of Hasidic women's head coverings in these terms, the distinct and ordered manifestations represent the level to which socialization has been embodied in precisely Hasidic fashion. The Hasidic woman who reveals no trace of hair whatsoever (no trace of the natural, libidinous forces of the inner body) epitomizes the ultimate in Hasidic socialization and piety. At the other extreme, is the woman who adorns only a wig, made from 100 percent 'natural' or human hair, without a covering. She embodies the closest representation to the unsocialized, uncontrolled forces of nature.

Thus, the more natural the composition of the *sheytl* and the more exposed the hair, the less Hasidic (or socialized, in Hasidic fashion) is the embodied display of the woman. Suri in fact discussed the hierarchical ordering of head coverings on a continuum from 'more Hasidish' to 'less Hasidish.' She defined the 'most Hasidish' form of head covering as embodied by those women who customarily wear a *tikhl* without any trace of hair, either synthetic or natural, exposed whatsoever-category (1). Reviewing the hierarchy in descending order, Suri reiterated, as an introduction to each new category, either, 'this one is less Hasidish' or 'this one is more modern.' In this case, 'modern' primarily translates as non-Hasidic or non-Jewish (like a non-Jew). The symbolic hierarchy thus descends from the most hyperbolized expression of Hasidic socialization and modesty, a form which leaves no doubt that every hair is covered and a women is indeed Hasidic, to the least hyperbolized expression, a wig made of 100 percent human hair, which could be in fact be mistaken for a woman's hair or perhaps the hair of any non-Jewish woman.

Lastly, this system of hierarchically ordered social distinctions may also be viewed in terms of distinct and stratified levels of Hasidic social control.

Fleeing centuries of persecution from the Christian majority, Jewish immigration was considerably different than that of other ethnic immigrant groups coming to the United States in the late nineteenth and early twentieth centuries. There was literally no turning back. Over two million Jews had emigrated from their European homes during the period of 1881-1924. In most European immigrant groups women comprised no more than a third of the entire group. However, almost half of the Eastern European Jewish immigrants were women. Jewish families came with the intention of making a new life in the United States.

In Russia (for example) Jews really made no effort to learn the dominant language . . . whereas in America . . . they set out at once to learn English with the aim of lessening the gulf between them and native born Americans (Heinze, 1990, p. 43).

In America, the New Jerusalem, a peculiar understanding emerged. This was a perverse sort of logical syllogism: If, just if, you could look like an American, you could be an American. If you could blend in, you could find peace. Style became emblematic, a characteristic not of fashion, not of appearance but of the soul and of loyalty to the new land. In America abundance was interpreted as paradisical plenty. Haven from persecution inter-animated with biblical utopia; this was, finally, the land of milk and honey. Secular portions of American life began to be interpreted in 'spiritual terms, viewing material existence as an integral part of the new Jerusalem' (Heinze, 1990, p. 90).

Since consumer capitalism was not antithetical to Jewish tradition, because of the material objects used in ritual worship, consumption just seemed to make sense. A variety of different historical threads fell into place, much like complex puzzle pieces, fitting together with much less difficulty than originally anticipated, creating a coherent picture. Jews, as I mentioned have always consecrated objects in ritual practices (you light the *Shabbat* Candles, you wear a *Tallis*, or a Yarmulke). Holidays never existed in name alone; holidays were always honored because they venerated the relationship (the covenant) with God. Holidays eventually re-signified the relationship with God into a relationship mediated by consumer capital.

Through the marketing of consumer goods, merchants re-signified and re-deployed the religious event as an occasion to shop. Indeed, in a setting that placed more emphasis on shopping than the veneration of religious rituals, the latter increasingly appeared as a rationale for the former (Heinze, 1990, p. 66). Consumption became inexorably intertwined with devotion and ultimately was privileged over devotion.

Jewish holidays blended into the fashion cycle, perhaps because the men who turned Seventh Avenue into the fashion industry were Jewish. Holidays that had little significance in the 'Old World' took on greater and greater significance in the new. Hanukkah (for example) was traditionally a minor Jewish holiday, but the holiday's proximity to the Christmas shopping season elevated the celebration's stature. The proximity shifted the base of the religious experience from 'partner in the divine convenant' (Heinze, 1990, p. 220), to partner in American Fordist practices.

Clothing as Democracy: A Strange Semiotic

Clothing worn in a world of global markets and mass marketing could eradicate differences. Framed by an appropriate package, anyone could be seen as anything. The uncomfortable memories of the Old World created a circumstance where the immigrants had an intense desire to fit in and become *American*. Understanding what was American however, may have been lost in translation. Newcomers wanted to believe, perhaps needed to believe, that after all that they had endured including crossing the Atlantic and coming to America, that the nation was open to them as a people. There was a sense the nation would embrace them only if they could become like and look like (their perceptions of) Americans.

Because in the ghettos where there was relatively little contact between the immigrants and 'Americans,' the use of the word 'perception' in the previous paragraph is quite operative. Reading the American body literally, body part by body part and setting it against the stereotypical text of 'The Jewish body,' the attempt was to adopt and adapt to American style, so the Jewish immigrant could be looked upon as an American, as belonging. Consumer culture encouraged the negotiation of 'social relationships with a calculating frame of mind' (Turner, 1996, p. 186). For, how the body is read and how the person is understood is established by 'the observing eye that reads it' (Turner, 1996, p. 229). A discerning eye could negotiate the symbolism and the codes and thus liberate him/herself from the yoke of centuries-old prejudices.

Irony on Seventh Avenue

Ironically, a large portion of the Jewish immigrant population worked in the fashion industry in production, wholesale and in retail, which helped create and sustain a continued interest in and focus on fashion. But Jewish cognizance and consciousness concerning what constituted American appearance standards stemmed from sensitivity and sensibility, a profound and pervasive desire for self-transformation and self-preservation. The Jewish population did become the dominant force in the fashion industry (and later in the movie industry). Thus perceptions of what was fashionable (a.k.a. American) was actually created by those who were trying to imitate 'the American.' The American in this light becomes a *simulacra*. The attention and concern of Jewish immigrants with American fashion cannot be read with a postmodern form of cynicism. It must be contextualized within an 'extraordinary . . . passionate commitment to American society.' (Heinze, 1990, p. 90). Fashion and consumption constituted the most easily accessible element of the new world. 'Clothes were as tangible as syntax was abstract and as obtainable as idioms were illusive.' (Heinze, 1990, p. 43).

Fashion and the American body became a form of study for Jewish immigrants. In traditional Judaism, the Talmud and the Torah are not to be read for precise meaning; rather, they are read problematically. The texts are meant to be studied, interpreted, theorized and (re)conceptualized. The *Kabbala*, the *Zohar* and other (cryptic) texts utilize numerology, astrology and complicated equations to arrive at new meanings and interpretations, which then subsequently give way to more questions. The American body was read with the same careful, critical, questioning probing eye.

A different form of orthodox worship emerged as tradition inter-animated with a social-semiotic reading of the secularized American environment. The understanding that America worshipped at the altar of social equity made it seem that democracy was manifested in the market. In the trope of the marketplace, clothing became the physical embodiment of this re-articulated form of worship. Fashion became a 'spiritual undertaking for Aliens striving for membership in a new society' (Heinze, 1990, p. 103). However, this material-spiritual dialectic also foreshadowed the transformation of the Jewish body.

The Godfather and an offer that could not be refused

In a sense 'America made an offer, huge numbers of Jews accepted: If they would accommodate the dominant culture by scrapping their foreign customs, they could become full partners in the American future' (McClain, 1995, p. 12). Appearance was and remains the signpost of difference. As McClain (1995, p. 34) noted visibility meant being seen as an outsider 'one of the ugly race . . . It is being visible in a body that betrays that the Jew is most uncomfortable.' One of the important themes taken up by the Yiddish press 'dwelled on the tantalizing idea of transforming one's self-image through the purchase of things' (Heinze, 1990, p. 103), part of a concerted effort to be less visibly different.

'They don't wear wigs here.' These were the words which Yekl, Abraham Cahan's 1896 fictional character greeted his wife when she stepped off the boat from Europe. She had joyfully put on the *shietel* [wig] to celebrate both the Sabbath and her reunion with her husband but, having become Americanized in the three years of their separation Yekl was painfully embarrassed by her appearance. (Gordon, 1995, p. 124) [Emphasis and definition added].

These visual cues were critical to Jewish immigrant women. Long before our foremothers were able to sound like Americans or even begin to speak a few words in broken English (let alone read) or 'much less fully negotiate the new culture' (Gordon, 1995, p. 118), they were encouraged to change their appearance by wearing brightly colored store bought clothing, hair-pieces, pointed shoes, flamboyant hats and even tightly bound high-waisted corsets. As Barbara Shierer explains, 'form preceded word' (Gordon, 1995, p. 118), perhaps more importantly form signified the word. Clothing became a fiction of American identity, a strategically deployed form of essentialism.

The Yiddish press, both newspapers and magazines (*Di Feyeb Velt* for example, the Jewish *Ladies Home Journal*) was specifically devoted to the transformed Jewish woman. The readers were blasted into both the industrial world 'and the consumer market' (Greene, 1994, p. 1245). Intensified consumerism places a price, an objective value on everything, even our bodies. Everything and everybody is ultimately cast into the market.

We shape and sustain our identities through objects. Anything that we consume must have some meaning in connection to a system of values. Clothing functions as a mode of communication. Much like language, appearance is read, translated and understood. Clothing 'helps people establish an identity as individuals and as members of a group' (Heinze, 1990, p. 90). Clothes do make the woman. Jane Addams (the founder of Hull House) observed many years ago (with both concern and cynicism) that:

young immigrant women spent 'money on clothes out of proportion to . . . her earnings. Clothes [become her] background [in the relative anonymity of the large American city] and from them she is largely judged' (Heinze, 1990, p. 103).

The person becomes a commodity by means of appropriate packaging, since, as Turner (1996, p. 122) noted, 'we no longer define' ourselves 'through blood or breeding. . . . Consumerism and the mass market . . . liquidated or at least blurred, the exterior marks of social and personal difference'.

the city, an American part of the city, she described herself as a 'slim figure of ardent youth . . . with dark age-old eyes that told of the restless seeking of her homeless race.' In fleeing that which she found contemptible, she made herself vulnerable to visibility. Yezierska exposed herself as someone who did not belong.

Consequently, Jewishness was okay, provided that you did not fit the image, or the stereotype of being Jewish. It became and remains a problematic identity to negotiate. What are the boundaries of a Jewish identity, or a Jewish body? How can the Jewish woman be Jewish if she has to be careful not to look Jewish, or sound Jewish, or act Jewish?

The Princess Paradox

Johnathan Flier, a Beverly Hills psychotherapist says:

> Our societal concept of beauty is not Jewish; it's Playboy, it's Glamour magazine, Cosmopolitan . . . Those aren't Jews on the cover; they may be Jewish, but they don't look Jewish. They're blonde, they have small noses, they have the hips, the body types that are generally not Jewish. So a lot of what becomes the prize . . . is defined by our society and it's not Jewish looking (McClain, 1995, p. 35)

Thus began a discourse of ambivalence, a series of clichés, which have tended to undergird the Jewish experience in the United States. This has been a complex and constantly contradictory terrain to negotiate. Our (Jewish) forefathers who created the fashion images of the perfect American body and the perfect American beauty, sent a message home to their Jewish wives and Jewish daughters that what was acceptable was not US. Hypothetically, even if the image looked like ourselves, we were never able to see our-selves in the image: the mirage and the barrage of smoke-screens and illusions. Jewish women constantly sought to conform, by transforming their bodies to correspond to the images that were created by their husbands, fathers and brothers. In order to fit in, to blend in, to appear and thus become American, to avert and insure that the prejudices of the past would not be visited on our bodies here, our Jewish bodies needed to melt into the melting pot; our bodies needed to disappear. But melting in did not come easily and it did not exact a tremendous cost. Jewish women consistently see themselves through a mirror of an over-abundance of deficiencies. As one woman explained I am 'too dark, hairy, curly headed, fat and big breasted.' The creators of the American fashion industry and Hollywood, Jewish men, seem to wish that the body of the Jewish woman would somehow just disappear altogether. A Jewish man explained:

The girls you wanted to go out with were the cheerleaders . . . I grew up during the Charlie's Angel's era, that's what you're looking for . . . none of Charlie's Angel's was Judy Weinberg (McClain, 1995, p. 35).

Another Jewish man concurred:

I am a fairly attractive Jewish boy, age twenty-five and I date only non Jewish girls . . . If someone would teach Jewish girls how to use make-up and look attractive . . . [things would be different]. Since there is no chance of that happening, I'm off to see my Korean girlfriend (McClain, 1995, p. 50).

A third stated:

American Jewish women, are crass, materialistic, neurotic, as opposed to non-Jewish women who are immediate, uncomplicated, unlayered, easy-going and fun loving . . . the girl in the Beer Commercial (McClain, 1995, p. 51).

A Jewish woman narrator (1995) internalized this saying:

I don't like those Polish Jewish rat faces do you? I mean those skinny faces with the long noses and the sunken eyes. I think they're ugly. My aesthetic is American. The ideal is the Dallas cowboy cheerleader (Annie Rophie in McClain, p. 34).

While still another woman exclaimed: 'What a compliment when someone says: 'You don't look Jewish!' Judith Weinstein Klein's doctoral work on Jewish identity and self-esteem suggests that being Jewish and being beautiful were mutually exclusive among Jewish women (McClain, 1993, p. 34). Daphene Merkin writes 'I have yet to meet a Jewish girl or woman who didn't take it as the highest accolade to hear it observed that she didn't look Jewish' (as quoted in McClain, 1993, p. 36). Descriptive terms such as cosmopolitan; aggressive; sophisticated; pushy; New York; exotic; ethnic; remain contentiously coded language, veiled ways of saying (in scatological sociological shorthand): 'Jewish.'

Shixas, Shylocks and Blondes

Two years ago a traveling art exhibition entitled 'Too Jewish' decided to take issue with what remained unsaid. What does it mean to be Jewish? What does it mean to look too Jewish? Is there a such a thing as Jewish beauty? Or, is it an oxymoron?

Noses are a case in point, Mittelman observed, pointing to Adam Rolston's series of drawings depicting rhinoplasty surgery – colloquially known as 'a nose job.' 'What he's talking about is the discomfort some Jews have with physical features that are too ethnic,' Mittelman said. 'We literally need to chop them away and get rid of our ethnicity.' Among the stereotypes confronted in 'Too Jewish?' is the image of the Jewish American Princess. One installation, Nurit Newman's 'Complex Princess,' relies on pink feathers and tiaras made from matzah meal to represent the torment the artist thinks princesses endure when trying to fit into the larger non-Jewish culture to which they can never truly belong. Another artistic take on the princess that evoked favorable response while on display in New York, Kleeblatt said, was 'Chanel Chanukah,' an unorthodox menorah made of nine Chanel lipsticks atop a quilted gold Chanel cosmetics bag (Arieff, 1997, p. 1).

The Chanel menorah (re)presents a form of religious fashion, fashioned religion and/or fashionable religion. It is a Jewish orthodoxy of the trans-formed Jewish body, a body that is still despised, but, a body that is despised more by our own brethren than anyone else (for who is more self-conscious of Jewishness in the United States than American Jews?). Fashion and religion inter-animate, becoming a consecrated practice of hiding those features, those things (including our names) which would reveal the body, as the Jewish body.

Growing up in the Bronx, Ralph Lifschitz attended the Talmudic Academy in Manhattan. . . . Today, Ralph Lauren reigns as the monarch of a fashion kingdom. 'I'm very Jewish,' says the designer, when asked how he feels about his religious and cultural background. 'Changing my name had nothing to do with being Jewish, people always assume it was because I don't like how Jewish it sounded, but that wasn't it at all. My identity is not something I wanted to change,' Lauren says. Lauren's personal style epitomizes American-ness in a quintessentially WASPish way. . . . The women are always slim-hipped, straight-haired, blond beauties with narrow noses. When asked whether he thinks there is any reflection of his religious background in his work, Lauren says 'no,' but that his style is no less Jewish than it is Protestant. After all, he says, 'what does Jewish look like?' (Cohen, 1996).

When we speak of Alicia Silverstone, or Lauren Bacall as Jews, we do so with that note of pride: 'you see they don't LOOK Jewish!' Well, if there is no such thing as a Jewish body, then why does it matter what Alicia Silver-stone and Lauren Bacall look like? What does their lack-of-Jewish-looks (re)present? Is it all smoke screens and mirrors and contrivances and distor-tions? We-ness is always defined in relation to others. Any sense of community exists because we believe it *does* exist. Our bodies are juxtaposed in relation to other bodies. Our sense of our bodies in juxtaposition also includes negative understandings that are strategically and agentically deployed. By saying there is no such thing as a Jewish body we engage in a form of resistance, a way to undermine dominant mythologies that sustain and shape particular power relations. While concurrently buying into the same power relations, we celebrate those bodies who do not appear to be Jewish.

A close friend of mine provided a narrative clue and a pragmatic explanation. She said, 'look at Alicia Silverstone – there is no such thing as a Jewish body. You can not tell who is really Jewish.' But, then she counters the previous narrative fragment with, 'Well, except at my daughter's pre-school. Now, there are so many throwbacks there. It is an embarrassment! ' What is the embarrassment? What are we trying to hide? What are the messages being sent? 'You know,' she said, 'the chubby Volvo and BMW set.' The 'I got to get my nails done and hair done set.' The 'there is a sale at Barney's set.'

Within the proliferation of multicultural and diversity arguments, within the *vive la difference* game, within the various tropes of identity, Jewish-ness is a confusion and a contradiction. Are we a culture? A religion? A race? None of the above? All of the above? We say Jews are white (now), we speak of a Judeo-Christian ethic (a new conflation to say the least), so, why do we [need] present ourselves as different? Why do we come off as different? How can we be part of the dominant group and the privileged group, if we are so different? To act too Jewish, to look too Jewish, plays with and betrays our new found privilege. What does too Jewish look like?

We live with a metaphorical scar. It is, however, a scar that is worn *fashionably.* Is it the scar that is worn, which asks us to conceal, that which in reality we can not reveal? One of my sisters asks that I don't let her boyfriend's parents know we are Jewish. My dear friend who wears her Judaism like a badge proudly states, 'my mother-in-law doesn't know I'm Jewish.' It would be different if her Judaism didn't matter to her, or perhaps to her mother in law. What my sister and my friend are articulating is a game of passing. They are pleased that they can pass. But, much like the tragic mulatta, what they seek was not theirs in the first place. Passing may be a dangerous game, a game of intrigue on the identity and image terrain. But, it is an ambivalent image that Jewish women and Jewish men negotiate. On one hand we want to be Jewish and we understand we are part of a group of people. Then on the other hand we celebrate being able to liberate ourselves from the stereotypical descriptors of the group. The following narrative highlights this clearly.

> I grew up thinking that Jewish meant shopping malls, hating nature and talking about non-Jews as the *goyim* . . . the Jews I knew seemed very shallow and materialistic . . . I associated so many negative qualities with Long Island Jews that I couldn't wait to leave. In college I was glad my blonde hair and blue eyes prevented me from looking Jewish (McClain, 1995, p. 31–2).

There is the myth-rumor-reality of the Jewish nose, the buxom Jewish girl, the accent (which is no longer East European, but New York). I recall the rite-of-passage in the gilded ghetto of my childhood, was not so much the *bat-mitzvah* but the nose job. McClain (1995) suggests Jewish women have a higher rate of eating disorders than among other groups. It is important to fit in, it is important not to let IT show. However, I am not sure what IT is. Yet, the changes are real. Is this part of a religious body or a class exigency?

> My mother often discussed how she would admire a WASP type of person, the way they dressed the way they conducted themselves. One New Jersey woman said 'and there was an undercurrent of how some people were so overbearingly Jewish that it was an embarrassment and that's why people have the stereotypes they do of the Jewish people because of that grotesque, obnoxious type of Jewish person (McClain, 1995, p. 31).

Several years ago, I was invited to go for a job interview to a predominately Jewish institution, with a predominately Jewish faculty in New York City. My mentor (an Irish-Catholic from Queens) felt it necessary to give me lessons in how to sound and act Jewish. To make a point of how important it was that I study 'Jewish-ness' she took me to several Jewish events where she passed as Jewish and I did not. Mother laughed about the whole thing, not without a certain amount of pride that her progeny melted so successfully into the pot (as I overheard her in conversation with her friend), 'that you couldn't even tell, even in a room full of Jews.'

A twenty-nine year old Jewish school teacher said the men she met at a Los Angeles synagogue all wanted the perfect little girl, the perfect tiny petite little thing whose hair was perfect, nails were perfect, Stepford wives . . . 'I always feel huge, I always feel awkward, I always feel ethnic.' (McClain, 1995, p. 36).

I do not want this chapter to descend into a discussion of the Jewish American Princess. She has been spoken about and written about, far too often. But she does need to be mentioned. The JAP, the Jewish American Princess is a classed body. She is the fashionably worn scar. The JAP speaks to a form of materialism, of conspicuous consumer consumption. The Jewish American Princess deflects these negative attributes away from both Jewish men and Gentile women. Obviously, anti-Semitism and misogyny cannot be reduced to a pedagogy of shopping or to a singular stereotype, that would be far too simplistic. Yet, it is the pervasiveness of the metaphor and the use of the stereotype by Jews themselves (particularly Jewish men) which is significant. No longer is the representation of the Jewish woman one of hard work or sacrifice. Rather, it is an image of wealth, superficiality, self-absorption and vacuousness. It is a representation of a trivialized albeit useless woman. You know that you are a JAP when:

> Neiman Marcus is #2 on your cellular's speed dial. You've had diamond studs soldered into your earlobes. You actually know the difference between carats and karats. Your dog owns more clothing and toys than your neighbor's children. (*The Jewish American Princess homepage* 1997).

Jewish womanhood in this contemporary conflation becomes both a market trope and a consumerist joke. What are three words a Jewish American Princess will never hear? Attention K-Mart Shoppers. You might be a Jewish American Princess 'if you only wear black clothes when you go out. If you are rich, Jewish and from Long Island. If you have a perfect nose that doesn't match your face. *(The Jewish American Princess homepage*, 1997). But if you don't wear the clothes, or adapt to the class exigencies then you are subjected to a different group of disparaging dictums. Contemporary Jewish woman-hood is a series of image-mines in our own minds, a 'damned if I do, damned if I don't' situation. Damned because the body of the Jewish female needs to disappear. The bodies of Jewish women are useless bodies if they are JAP bodies and bodies that betray the Americanization of Jewry if they are not.

So, I sit here at my computer – the heiress to a rapidly disappearing body. A body that began in the strength of women who refused to let their children die, who crossed the Atlantic bravely, facing a new universe and a new world. I am a body conceived not in Liberty, but in commodity and dedicated to the muted pastels that dot the American landscape of homogenization from sea to shining sea (where each and every mall has a Gap). A body transformed by a desire to fit in, which ended up in images of deprecatory derision and scorn. A body that loses by concealing, that which under no circumstances ought be revealed.

Ethnicity (whatever that unit of measure is), white-ness (an illusive unit of measure by which everything else is evaluated) and a plethora of other categories that paradigmaticize processes, ultimately (re)create culture as a thing, an object a commodity. The body becomes the receptacle of a series of physical markers, of objective ethnic characteristics, a caricature, an imitation, a parody.

Back to the Beach

I end where I begin, on the beach, the fun and sun capital of the world, my home. I think back to the faces and images of family and friends. My best friend tried to teach me that in order to fit in I ought to sleep with my nose on a pillow and that way it would slowly conform and reform itself and that way I wouldn't look too Jewish. My father told me there was no such thing as someone who looked Jewish, that it was all a myth. But, he also said that *shixsas* (a disparaging term for non-Jewish women) had no chins and skinny legs. None of the Jewish boys who were my playmates growing up, now transformed into sensitive, caring, non-sexist men (my tongue remains firmly ensconced in my cheek), married Jewish women. Many of them grew up in religious households. I ask why? I might have just listened to Jerry Seinfeld for the answer which was: 'shixsappeal.' The forbidden fruit, the legitimizing factor, the blonde that can not betray.

I do see transformation. My grandmother was four feet ten inches tall, my sister is a foot taller than she was, as a result of nutrition and vitamins. I see our elongated lankiness in stark contrast to the images of Jewish immigrant women. First our bodies immigrated, then we conformed to fashion. I see nose jobs, breast jobs and a profound array of eating disorders. But there is something else, something that remains an enigma to me. Fashion and images transformed the body, but what remains, what is left, is self-hatred and scorn. For what we are and for what we will never be (as we negotiate the minefield of illusory images), are caught up in a nightmare of our own construction and our own desires to fit into the larger American society. I look around me and try to find something that is identifiably Jewish about US. What I find is that we try so hard not to look Jewish, that we become even *more* Jewish in our attempt to conform to an American myth. We become impersonators, we invoke a sense of performance, of drag. We have mastered the look and the nuances, but like the swamp gas that rises in the morning from the Everglades, what we seek never was really there in the first place.

My son asks: 'What do you want to do mom?' I answer, 'go shopping.' For me, as the heiress to the tradition, it is my sacrament, my consecrated practice, my identity and my understanding of who and what I am. I remember Mama as I pray in the car: 'please, please do not let dinner go to my thighs, and please let me wear a size four, please, please . . .'

References

Arieff, D. (1997) Too jewish. Jewish Journal of Greater Los Angeles. Available on the web at http//:www.aol.com.jewishcommunity/artexhibit or ab871@lafn.org.

Azoulay, K. (1997). *Black, jewish and interracial*. Durham, N.C. Duke University Press.

Cabot, V. (1996). American jews – or jewish americans? In the *Scottsdale Jewish Bulletin*. Available at: http://www.aol.com/jewishcommunity/scotsdale.

Cohen, D. (1996). In the eye of the beholder: Jewish identity through a lens. In the *Jewish Telegraphic Agency*. Available at: http://www.aol.com/jewishcommunity/lauren.

Dettelbach, C. (1996). Faces in the jewish mirror. In the *Cleveland Jewish Press* (12/20/96). Available at http:www.aol.com/jewishcommunity/bacall.

Falk, P. (1994). *The consuming body*. Thousand Oaks, California: Sage.

Gilman, S. (1991). *The Jew's body*. New York: Routledge.

Gordon, B. (1995). 'They don't wear wigs': issues and complexities in the development of an exhibition. *American Quarterly, 47* (March, 1995), pp. 116–36.

Greene, V. (1994). 'Becoming American women: clothing and the Jewish immigrant experience (1880–1920) *The Journal of American History, 81* (December 1994): 1243–7.

Gross, N. (1996). I love you but I can't afford you. In the *Jerusalem Post* (12/26/96). Available at: http:www.aol.com/jewishcommunity/wigs.

Heinze, A. (1990) *Adapting to abundance*, New York: Columbia University Press.

Jewish American Princess homepage. (1997). Available: http://www.gate.net~pogrom.

McClain E. (1995). *Embracing the other*. New York: Basic Books.

Turner, B. (1996). *The body in society*. Thousand Oaks, CA: Sage.

Weinberg, S. (1988). *The world of our mothers*. Chapel Hill, NC: University of North Carolina Press.

Yezierska, A. (1923) *Children of loneliness*. New York: Funk and Wagnalls.

Index